THE *BIMBAMĀNA*

Bibliotheca Indo-Buddhica Series
Sunil Gupta, Editor

Bibliotheca Indo-Buddhica Series—No. 138.

Buddhist Iconometry

The *Bimbamāna* of Gautamīyaśāstra

As heard by Śāriputra

Edited and translated into English
by
E.W. Marasinghe

Sri Satguru Publications
A Division of
Indian Books Centre
Shakti Nagar, Delhi - India

Published by:
Sri Satguru Publications
A Division of
Indian Books Centre,
Oriental & Indological Publishers
40/5, Shakti Nagar,
Delhi - 110 007.
INDIA

First Edition: Delhi, 1994

ISBN 81-7030-417-2

PRINTED IN INDIA

Contents

Preface

Among the topics discussed in Sanskrit *śilpa* texts iconometry occupies an important place. Indian *śilpa* texts such as *Mānasāra, Śilparatna, Kāśyapaśilpa, Kāmikāgama* and *Vaikhānasāgama* describe in detail the measurements pertaining to statues of Hindu gods and goddesses. But only a handful of Indian *śilpa* texts that deal with the iconometry of Buddha images have come down to us. The *Pratimāmānalakṣaṇa* and the *Samyaksambuddha-bhāṣita-pratimālakṣaṇa* are two such works which treat of the subject of Buddhist iconometry in some detail. But it is noteworthy that the two hitherto known Sanskrit *śilpa* texts which deal with Buddhist iconometry quite comprehensively belong to no other country than Sri Lanka.

Of these two *śilpa* texts the *Māñjuśrībhāṣita-vāstuvidyāśāstra* (also called *Citrakarmaśāstra*) is a unique work devoted to Buddhist monastic architecture and imagecraft including iconometry, iconography and related topics in some 1600 *ślokas*. The only available MS. of this work has now been edited and published together with an English translation, in two volumes (in Bibliotheca Indo-Buddhica Series, Delhi, India).

The other work, the *Bimbamāna*, popularly known as *Śāriputra*, must be a few centuries posterior to the *Vāstuvidyāśastra*, and most probably belong to the 11th or 12th century. This work exclusively deals with the iconometry of standing, sedent and recumbent Buddha images in accordance with the superior ten-*tāla* system. It seems that it has come down as a useful manual which has been preserved among families of traditional temple artists in Sri Lanka from ancient times up to the present day. This is also borne out by the fact that no less than fifteen complete manuscripts, all except one on palmleaf, have been discovered in Sri Lanka. However, it is doubtful whether the artisans who did not possess a sufficient knowledge of Sanskrit were able to fully comprehend the many instructions given and meticulous specifications laid down in the text. The word-to-word commentary in Sinhala is, in most cases, nothing but a repetition in syntactical order of the Sanskrit terms with 'Sinhalized' endings. It might, therefore, have been absolutely necessary for an artisan to receive guidance under an expert teacher.

An English translation of this important *śilpa* text based on a critical edition had been a long-felt need. The only Sri Lankan edition which has appeared in Sinhala script is that by Rev. M. Sirivimala published in 1924 under the title *Śāriputra sravaṇo Bimbapramāṇam*. This edition contains 126 *ślokas*. However, it is not a critical edition but, as the editor himself admits, only a reproduction of the text according to a single manuscript with only a few illegible letters being supplied by the editor. The text is accompanied by the verse-to-verse commentary in Sinhala. Although the editor had promised to bring out a second part of the text which he apparently had in his possession, it never appeared.

In his *Mediaeval Sinhalese* Art, Ananda Coomaraswamy published an incomplete translation of about 100 verses from the *Śāriputra*, supplied to him by one Mudaliyar E.W. Gooneratne of Galle. The copy used by this gentleman for his translation apparently had two parts, the latter part being the same as the text now available on palmleaf. The first part dealing with a system of inferior measure with details of plumb-line measurements is no longer available. It is not clear whether the section referred to by Mr. Gooneratne is the same as that mentioned by Rev. Sirivimala. However, the contents of all the available MSS. of the *Bimbamāna*, with the exception of a few *ślokas*, remain consistently the same.

Fifty years after the appearance of its first edition, Hans Ruelius produced a critical edition of the *Śāriputra* together with another shorter Sanskrit work on iconometry called *Ālekhyalakṣaṇa*, accompanied by a German translation of both works, for his Ph.D. degree of the University of Göttingen. This edition was based on twelve manuscripts including one hand-written copy. One palmleaf manuscript in the possession of the British Museum Library is written in Grantha characters, which appears to be the oldest while all the rest are in Sinhalese cursive script. This edition contains 139 verses.

Ruelius' edition has several noteworthy features. It is the first critical edition of this important *śilpa* text. Not only the Sanskrit text but also its commentary in Sinhala has been edited. The several very important and carefully drawn figures illustrating the measurements given in the text of the three types of Buddha image enhance the value of the publication.

However, Ruelius' edition is not free from defects. The amended text differs from the MSS. in many instances. The editor appears to have aimed at a cleaner text free from metrical defects and grammatical errors. But we should not forget that metrical and grammatical flaws and ambiguity are defects shared by all Sanskrit *śilpa* texts, and any attempt to correct all such defects would tantamount to complete distortion of the original text. The task of the editor of a Sanskrit *śilpa* text should be to restore the original text as faithfully as possible, without trying to rid it of all such defects. However, justice should be done to Ruelius by stating here that he has indicated in his notes all his amendments to the text.

Ruelius takes the total height of the *uttama-daśa-tāla* figure as set out in the *Śāriputra* to be 125 *dehāṅgulas*. This goes against the injunction of the *śilpa* text itself that the total height of an *uttama-daśa-tāla* statue should measure 124 *aṅgulas*. This extra inch is the result of Ruelius' taking the *bhāga* constantly to mean 4½ *aṅgulas*, thereby making the knee and the foot 4½ *aṅgulas* each. But either of these parts measures 4 *aṅgulas* according to all *śilpa* texts. It must be remembered that, although the *Śāriputra* prescribes the *bhāga* to be 4½ *aṅgulas*, in actual practice it sometimes stands for 4 *aṅgulas* instead of 4½ *aṅgulas*. The *Citrakarmaśāstra* in fact always takes the *bhāga* as four and not 4½ *aṅgulas*. In the present work, in *Śloka* 53, the vertical distance from the hiccup-line to the armpit is given as two *bhāgas*, which should actually be eight *aṅgulas*, as confirmed by other *śilpa* texts. The *bhāga* given as the height of the knee and of the foot should also be construed in the same way.

I am also unable to accept Ruelius' interpretation of '*viṁśatiścāpi māntran tu*' in *Śloka* 28 as twenty *aṅgulas*. '*Mātra*' here stands for '*aṅgula*' and the use of '*cāpi*' is very significant. It should, therefore, be understood as 'twenty and one *aṅgulas*' and not just 'twenty *aṅgulas*'. In fact the length of the hand of an *uttama-daśa-tāla* figure according to all *śilpa* texts is twenty-one *aṅgulas*. His calculation of the number of hair locks on the Buddha's head as 317 is again erroneous. He takes '*arkaśśara*' in '*arkaśśaraśasatatrayam*' (*Śloka* 32) as 12 + 5 even disregarding the commentator's interpretation as 12 x 5, which should be the correct one. Thus the total number of hair locks should be 360 and not 317.

The present edition is based on two palmleaf manuscripts in the possession of the Library of University of Peradeniya, which have escaped notice of Ruelius who used for his edition twelve other manuscripts, all from Sri Lanka. These two manuscripts are for the most part in perfect condition and almost complete save for a few initial lines missing from either copy. The MS. bearing No. 277495 is given as 'क' in this edition and the copy bearing No. 277340(1) called 'ग'. Although I have also examined a number of manuscript copies in the possession of the British Museum Library and the Colombo Museum Library, some of them in microfilm, I have used only Ruelius' edition which incorporates them all. It is indicated by the letter 'च' in this edition. The other edition compared here is that of M. Sirivimala Thera brought out in 1924. This is the only edition printed in Sri lanka and can be regarded as another copy of the *Bimbamāna* as the editor himself confesses that it is the reproduction of a single manuscript with only a few illegible letters here and there being supplied by him. It is indicated by the letter 'अ' in this edition.

Ruelius has largely amended the text mainly for grammatical and metrical considerations. Of these amendments what I considered plausible have been accepted in the present edition without acknowledgment, but such instances can be noted by comparing the text with his amendments he has given along with other variant readings in his notes. The amendments I have rejected are given in the footnotes under 'च'.

A critical edition and an English translation of this important *śilpa* text have been a long-felt need and, and it is hoped that the present volume will satisfy that need. The translation is literal and verse-to-verse. The words and phrases given within square brackets are the translator's own and would serve to make the translation perfect and more readable. The words within parentheses are only further explanations of the word/s that immediately precede.

Lack of a proper knowledge of this ancient science of iconometry has resulted in our present day artisans creating objects bereft of artistic excellence, that can hardly match such masterpieces as the famous *samādhi* image and those seated images at Pankuliya and Toluvila at Anurādhapura. However, our research has revealed that Buddha images belonging to the Anurādhapura period have been sculptured in accordance with the iconometric system set out in the *Citakaramaśāstra* and that the sculpture of the Polonnaruva Period has been influenced by the tenets of the *Bimbamāna*. Nevertheless, these two works, the *Bimbamāna* and the *Citrakarmaśāstra*, provide invaluable information on ancient Buddhist iconometry, which can be used to great advantage by modern Buddhist sculptors in Sri Lanka and elsewhere.

Acknowledgements

I wish to record my deep gratitude to Mr. Aryaratne Senadeera, Librarian of the University of Peradeniya, for granting me the necessary permission to consult the two palmleaf manuscripts on which the present edition is based, the staff of the same Library for their expert and valuable assistance, Mr. Ananda Gunasinghe, Head of the Department of Languages and Cultural Studies, University of Sri Jayewardenepura, for his salutary advice and Mr. Saman Chandra Ranasinghe, Visiting Lecturer in Sanskrit, and Mr. Ratnasiri Arangala, Lecturer in Sinhala of the same University, who obliged by reading the proofs through.

Finally I must say a special word of thanks to Mr. Naresh Gupta and Mr. Sunil Gupta of Sri Satguru Publications for the interest they took to publish this edition in their prestigious Bibliotheca Indo-Buddhica Series.

University of Sri Jayewardenepura, E.W.M.
Nugegoda,
Sri Lanka.
1st October, 1993.

Introduction

The text of the *Bimbamāna* begins quite unceremoniously with the words '*athedānīm pravakṣyāmi*' (I shall now expound), and this would suggest that it is only a detached chapter from a larger work, separately edited with a Sinhala commentary for the benefit of temple artists. Unfortunately, the original work appears to have perished or is yet to be discovered. We do not know for certain how it was called but the phrase '*gautamīye śāriputraśrute bimbamānam*' found in the colophons of certain manuscripts suggests that it bore a title like *Gautamīyaśāstra* which ascribed the authorship to Gautama the Buddha from whose mouth it was heard by Śāriputra (*śāriputraśruta*), the Buddha's chief disciple. This prompts us to associate the work with the Theravāda School which would make the possibility of its having been written in Sri Lanka stronger. Certain manuscripts, however, have the colophon '*iti gautamīye śāriputraśrute bimbamānam samāptam*' followed by a *mantra* containing the name of Akṣobhya Tathāgata (*akṣotbhava-tathāgata*), but we cannot attach much importance to it because the *mantra* could be a later addition done by a scribe according to his personal predilection.

Tissa Kariyavasam refers to an ola-leaf manuscript of the *Śāriputra* (copied from an earlier copy in 1902) which contains an appendix entitled *Devasthāpanaya* running to 22 *ślokas*. It sets out the auspicious times for the installation (*sthāpanā*) of a deity (*deva*) and lists the benefits of adhering to auspicious times and consequences of violating the *śāstras*. This however appears to be a later addition which has nothing to do with the *Śāriputra*. By '*deva*' most probably a Hindu god is meant although the phrase '*pratimācakṣuḥ-karaṇe*' occurring in the final stanza has been interpreted by the commentator as 'in the case of the painting of the eyes of the Buddha image'.

The subject-matter of the *Bimbamāna*, as its name indicates, is confined to the iconometry of Buddha images. The subject of iconometry covers two areas, the plumbline measurements and the measurements of the image itself. The plumbline measurements are taken along a number of plumblines suspended from a wooden frame known as '*lambaphalaka*' (Sinh. *lamba-taṭuva*), hung above the image being modelled or carved. There may be nine or eleven plumblines suspended in front of the image at various points and five or seven behind it. The image takes shape between these two sets of plumblines. Of these the middle line in front (*madhyasūtra*) is suspended dividing the image into two symmetrical halves. It thus falls along the middle of the forehead, the meeting-place of the eye-brows, the tip of the nose, the middle of the lips, in between the breasts, along the navel and the penis and through the thighs, knees, shanks and the feet. The remaining plumblines are suspended at various points on either side of the *madhyasūtra*. Thus two lines fall along the extremity of the face, two along the outer edge of the ear, another set through the arm-pits and another just outside the two arms. A fifth set is sometimes suspended between the last two *sūtras* and falls along the middle of the arms.

The plumblines are also used for determining the elevation of the various parts of the image. For example, the tip of the nose is taken to be one *aṅgula* behind the *madhyasūtra*. Similarly the distances between these lines and the important points that are immediately behind them should be carefully noted.

The second type of measurement covers all those measurements taken along the body of the image. They are of five kinds, namely, *māna*, *pramāṇa*, *parimāṇa*, *unmāna* and *upamāna*. The *māna* refers to the vertical measurements such as the distance from the hair-limit to the eye-line, from that point to the tip of the nose, the length of the arms and of the legs and so on. The *pramāṇa* means the horizontal measurements or the breadth, for instance, the distance between the two shoulders, the width of the body at chest level, the width of the belly or the width of the arm or of the thigh. The circumference or girth is referred to as *parimāṇa*, for instance, the girth of the arm or of the thigh, the thickness of the nipple of the breasts. The *unmāna* is the measurement of the elevation or height, such as the height of the nipple or of the breasts or of the tube of the nose. The *upamāna* is the measurement of interspaces, i.e., the width of the navel, the interval between the two thighs or the two big toes. These five kinds of measurement taken together with the plumbline measurements constitute the six kinds of iconometric measurement as applied to standing, seated and reclining images.

The Place and the Date of the Work

The *Bimbamāna* presents the best in-depth study of the iconometric system of superior ten-*tāla* (*uttama-daśa-tāla*) as applied to the making of Buddha images. There are, however, other Sanskrit *śilpa* texts which treat of the subject of *uttama-daśa-tāla* in fair detail. Some of the best known among them are the *Kāmikāgama, Aṁśumadbhedāgama, Vaikhānasāgama, Ajitāgama, Śilparatna, Kāśyapaśilpa* and the *Mānasāra*. But all these works have reserved the superior ten-*tāla* measure for the highest of the Hindu gods, namely, Brahmā, Viṣṇu and Śiva. Another very early work on iconometry which has a Buddhist flavour was edited and published together with an English translation by Phanindranath Bose in 1929 under the title *Pratimā-māna-lakṣaṇa*. Evidently an abridged version of a larger work called *Atreyatilaka*, a copy of it had been presented to the Viśvabhāratī University library during the time of Rabindranath Tagore, and it was the copy that was used by Bose for his edition. The work containing 143 stanzas deals with the iconometric systems of *navatāla, aṣṭatāla, saptatāla* and *ṣaṭtāla* before the *daśatāla* which is dismissed in barely eight verses. It is followed by the *saptatāla* again and *catustāla* and a discourse on the disposal of damaged statues (*jīrṇoddhāra*). According to this work, the *daśatāla* system is used for measuring images of Brahmā, Carcikā Goddess, Brahma-Rākṣasas, of divine beings and of the Buddhas. It appears that the system described is the *madhyama-daśatāla*, as the number of units the image is made up of is one hundred and twenty and the thighs and the shanks measure twenty-six *aṅgulas* each.

The iconometric system set out in the *Pratimāmana-lakṣaṇa* differs widely from that of the *Bimbmāna*. And it does not seem to have been meant exclusively for Buddha images, for no provision is made for the *uṣṇīṣa* which is one of the characteristic features of a Buddha image. The buttocks and the hips together make fourteen instead of thirteen *aṅgulas*, the knee five *aṅgulas* and the feet three *aṅgulas*, thus precluding the possibility of one work influencing the other. And no manuscript of the *Bimbamāna* has been discovered anywhere in India. All the manuscripts (numbering over fifteen) so far found are from Sri Lanka.

Ven. Kamburupitiye Vanaratana is inclined to think that the *Bimbamāna* and two other works, the *Samyaksambuddhabhāṣita-pratimālakṣaṇa* discovered in India and the *Śāriputra-sūtra* mentioned in the Tibetan sources belong to one and the same Vajrayāna School. I however find it difficult to succumb to this view, for the *Bimbamāna* rather appears to be a work compiled in Sri Lanka taking into consideration the local needs, although Indian influence on it can by no means be ruled out. The absence of the mention of the seated and recumbent images in the other two works and the fact that all the extant copies of the *Bimbamāna* are those discovered from Sri Lanka lead us towards that conclusion. Although it may have originally belonged to the Vajrayāna School, as Ven. Vanaratana rightly observes, the compiler of the work has been careful not to allow his exposition of the *śāstra* to come into conflict with the local Theravāda tradition. There is no mention of the Sambhogakāya Buddhas and Bodhisattvas and of the Mahāyānic rites and rituals. This may be the reason for the popularity it enjoys in Sri Lanka up to the present day. The *Mañjuśrī-Citrakarmaśāstra*, on the other hand, being boldly Mahāyānic in character, seems to have lost its popularity with the decline of Mahāyānism in Sri Lanka.

Nevertheless, the *Bimbamāna's* affinity to the *Citrakarmaśāstra* in style and treatment is too strong to be ignored. The latter work dealing with Buddhist monastic architecture and imagecraft is strangely titled differently in its two sections treating of the two subjects, i.e., *Vāstuvidyāśāstra* and *Citrakarmaśāstra* respectively. In all probability it was written before the 7th century A.C. The *Bimbamāna* is definitely posterior to this work and there is a strong possibility of the former work being influenced by the latter, eventhough there are minor divergencies between the traditions represented in the two works. The language of the *Bimbamāna* is much closer to that of the *Citrakarmaśāstra* than to those of the South Indian works, almost all of them written around the 10th century and after. But the language of the *Bimbamāna* is decidedly more sophisticated and it also contains a few verses couched in more complicated metres like Indravajrā, Upendravajrā and Upajāti.

The *Citrakarmaśāstra* treats of the subject of iconometry in three separate chapters. In one (Chapter 8) it lays down the measurements of the *śūla* or wooden image-core belonging to the three types of *daśatālamāna* with detailed descriptions of its various component parts. In Chapter 14 the three varieties of *daśa-tāla-māna* are described one by one in relation to an standing image. The next chapter deals with the application of the plumbline measurements together with the description of sedentary images. No reference to recumbent images is found in the *Citrakarmaśāstra*. It knows of only two types of image, the standing and the sedentary. The recumbent image is definitely a later development. This also points to the later date of the *Bimbamāna* which gives an expert's exposition of the iconometry of a reclining image. The *Bimbamāna* omits the *madhyama-daśa-tāla* and the *kaniṣṭhadaśa-tāla* but presents a much more detailed treatment of the *uttama-daśatāla* measure, the plumbline measurements, the seated image and the reclining image. It appears that the *Bimbamāna* is an improved version of the latter two chapters of the *Citrakarmaśāstra*.

Unlike in the case of the *Citrakarmaśāstra* we are fortunate in having a large number of manuscripts of the *Bimbamāna*. Of these the earliest one is undoubtedly the one in Grantha script now kept in the British Museum Library. This manuscript of the Sanskrit text and the gloss in Sinhala can be dated as far back as the 12th century A.C., which would push the date of the original composition of the work at least to the 11th century.

The *Citrakarmaśāstra* and the *Bimbamāna*.

Although there are vestiges of the *Bimbamāna* being influenced by the *Citrakarmaśāstra*, if we examine the two works closely, it will be seen that they represent two different traditions. Apart from the numerous discrepancies in the iconometric systems set out in the two works, there are other differences between them, which make it difficult to associate them with one particular tradition. The main points of departure may be given as follows.

(a) The *āyādiṣaḍvarga* formulas described in the two works differ in the following details. The two works, agree only with regard to three of them, that is, the *yoni*, the *nakṣatra* and the *āya*. According to the *Bimbamāna* the *aṃśaka* is obtained by multiplying the desired measurement by eight and dividing the result by nine. But according to the *Citrakarmaśāstra* it is the *nakṣtra*-remainder that is multiplied by eight and not the desired measurement. The *vyaya* as given in the *Vāstuvidyāśāstra* is obtained by multiplying the desired measurement by three but according to the *Citrakarmaśāstra* and the *Bimbamāna* the multiplier is nine. In both these cases the result is divided by fourteen. The *Bimbamāna* differs from the *Vāstuvidyāśāstra* by making the dividing factor ten instead of fourteen. In the *vāra* the desired measurement is multiplied by 10 according to the *Citrakarmaśāstra*, by nine according to the *Bimbamāna*.

(b) Whereas the *Citrakarmaśāstra* deals with only the standing and sedentary images, the *Bimbamāna* deals with the iconometry of all three types of images, standing, sedentary and recumbent.

(c) The *Bimbamāna* makes greater use of enigmatic language as can be seen from expressions like '*īśāvatārabhānuś ca mārgadharmartus tatkramāt*' (Verse 65).

(d) According to the *Bimbamāna* eleven plumblines were suspended in front and nine at the back of the image being modelled. The *Citrakarmaśāstra* speaks of only nine plumblines in front and five behind.

(e) The *Bimbamāna* uses the word *bhāga* generally to mean a length of 4½ *aṅgulas* while the *Citrakarmaśāstra* always takes it to mean four *aṅgulas*.

All these suggest that the treatment of the subject of iconometry in the *Bimbamāna* is more sophisticated than that outlined in the *Citrakarmaśāstra*, which fact may point to the later date of the former work.

Since the *Citrakarmaśāstra* and the *Bimbamāna* are the only two comprehensive works on Buddhist iconometry, it would be worthwhile to make a short comparative study of the various measurements set out in the two works. The *Bimbamāna* deals with only the superior ten-*tāla* system where the face-length is given as 13½ *aṅgulas*. The total height of the standing image, therefore, consists of 9.2 (124 ÷ 13½) face-lengths. A face-length according to the *Citrakarmaśāstra* measures $13^1/_8$ *aṅgulas* (i.e., 3 *yavas* less than that in the *Bimbamāna* and the total height of the image is thus made up of 9.45 face-lengths (124 ÷ $13^1/_8$).

I have compared the iconometric measurements given in the two works with those furnished by certain Hindu *śilpa* texts, in tabulated form, in my Introduction to the *Citrakarmaśāstra Ascribed to Mañjuśrī*. Some of the striking differences between the two systems are as follows:

The vertical measurements (*māna*) from the *uṣṇīṣa* to the end of the jaw-limit are totally different. As far as these measurements are concerned, the *Bimbamāna* is in perfect agreement with the *Kāmikāgama*, a South Indian *śilpa* text, while the *Citrakarmaśāstra* totally agrees with the *Śilparatna*. Thus the *uṣṇīṣa* in the *Bimbamāna* measures one *aṅgula* which is three *yavas* less than that in the *Citrakarmaśāstra*. The distance from the bottom of the *uṣṇīṣa* to the end of the hair-limit in front is identical in the two works, i.e., three *aṅgulas*. The face from the hair-limit to the jaw-limit is divided into three equal parts, namely from the hair-limit to the eye-line, from the eye-line to the nose-tip and from there to the jaw-limit, each measuring 4½ *aṅgulas* according to the *Bimbamāna* and one *yava* less (i.e., 4³/₈ *aṅgulas*) according to the *Citrakarmaśāstra*. Below that point the vertical measurements are identical in the two works. This shows that the difference lies in the depiction of the face, the *Bimbamāna* statue having a slightly elongated face compared with that described in the *Citrakarmaśāstra*.

Slight variations are also noticeable in the horizontal measurements including those taken along the surface of the body. Of these the most important divergences pertain to the length of the eye which is three *aṅgulas* in the *Bimbamāna* and two *aṅgulas* in the other, and to the length of the mouth which is four *aṅgulas* in the former and two *aṅgulas* and four and a half *yavas* in the latter.

These horizontal measurements are also useful in determining the positions of the plumblines that are suspended in front of and behind the image being modelled, for the texts do not give their exact positions in terms of *aṅgulas*. They only mention the various parts of the body which should fall behind each plumbline. Thus the *madhyasūtra* or the middlemost line falls along the meeting-place of the eye-brows, in front of the nose, along the navel and the generative organ and through the knees and the legs, dividing the image into two symmetrical halves. The *pārśvasūtra* which is suspended on either side of the *madhyasūtra* falls along the extremity of the face, by the side of the neck, through the breast and the middle of the foot. Of these points the middle of the breast is the most important. Elsewhere it is said that the distance from the hiccup to the nipple of the breast is 13½ *aṅgulas* and that the same shall be the distance between the nipples of the breasts, thus an imaginary line joining the two breasts and the hiccup forming a perfect isosceles triangle each side measuring 13½ *aṅgulas*. The two *pāśvasūtras* are therefore suspended thirteen and a half *aṅgulas* apart.

The only clue that can be taken for determining the position of the next plumbline which is called *karṇasūtra* (or ear-line) is the width of the ear which is given as two *aṅgulas.* Thus either *karṇasūtra* is suspended at a distance of two *aṅgulas* from the *pārśvasūtra.* According to the *Citrakarmaśāstra,* however, the ear measures two *aṅgulas* and two *yavas* at the *pippalī* which pushes the *karṇasūtra* two *yavas* further from the *pārśvasūtra* making the distance between the two *sūtras* 18 *aṅgulas* as against 17½ in the *Bimbamāna.*

The next line is the *kakṣasūtra* which falls through the armpit, by the side of the hip, outside the calf and by the side of the little toe. Both the *Bimbamāna* and the *Citrakarmaśāstra* agree on the distance between the two armpits which is 22½ *aṅgulas*. This makes the distance between the *karṇasūtra* and the *kakṣasūtra* 2½ *aṅgulas* in one and 2¼ *aṅgulas* in the other. There is no proper clue that would help us determine the position of the *kakṣabāhyasūtra* which is described as falling along the middle of the arm and by the side of the foot. But the position of the *bāhusūtra* which falls along the outer edge of the arm can be determined with certainty for the work says that the width of the body at the shoulders (*bāhuvistāra*) is forty and a half *aṅgulas*. This would make the distance between the *kakṣasūtra* and the *bāhusūtra* nine *aṅgulas*, and judging from the pattern that has been followed in positioning the other plumblines it would be reasonable to assume that the *kakṣabāhyasūtra* was suspended at a distance of 4½ *aṅgulas* from either line.

In keeping with the larger contour of the face, the other horizontal measurements pertaining to the face slightly differ from those given in the *Citrakarmaśāstra*. For example, the distance from the crown (*uṣṇīṣa*) to the hair-limit in front and at the back is 10.0 *aṅgulas* and 13½ *aṅgulas* respectively as against 9½ and 12½ *aṅgulas* as given in the *Citrakarmaśāstra*. The distance between the two ears in front is 22.0 *aṅgulas* in one and 21½ *aṅgulas* in the other. There is no difference between the distance between the two ears at the back.

The other major discrepancies in measurement pertain to the torso. In the *Bimbamāna* the width of the torso at chest level and that of the waist in front are identical while the *Citrakarmaśāstra* describes a slightly slenderer body with the chest measuring 16½ *aṅgulas* and the waist 17½ *aṅgulas.*

There is also a slight difference in the positioning of the two feet in the two traditions. The *Bimbamāna* prescribes the interspace between the two big toes to be six *aṅgulas* while it is eight *aṅgulas* according to the *Citrakarmaśāstra.* The distance between the two thighs is given as one *aṅgula* in both works but the gap between the legs gradually widens in the latter work with the distance between the two knees being three *aṅgulas* and that between the two ankles 5½ *aṅgulas* as against two *aṅgulas* and four *aṅgulas* respectively in the former.

The foregoing would amply demonstrate that the two works the *Bimbamāna* and the *Citrakarmaśāstra* represent two distinctly different iconometric traditions that obtained in ancient Sri Lanka, and we may even hazard the suggestion that they must have been used as manuals separately by the artisans belonging to the two Schools, the Theravāda and the Mahāyāna.

शारिपुत्रश्रुते गौतमीयशास्त्रे बिम्बमानम्

The *Bimbamāna* of Gautamīyaśāstra as heard by Śāriputra

अथ
शारिपुत्रश्रुते गौतमीये
बिम्बमानम्।

[बिम्बानां त्रयो भेदाः।]

अथेदानीम् प्रवक्ष्यामि बिम्बमानविधिं शृणु[1] ।
निषण्णस्थितशयितेन[2] त्रिविधं सम्प्रकल्पयेत् ।।१।।

[बिम्बद्रव्याणि।]

यद्बिम्बे च कृते द्रव्यं स्वर्णं ताम्रन्तु मृण्मयम् ।
शैलकाष्ठेष्टिकाचूर्णं[3] बिम्बं तत्र प्रवक्ष्यते[4] ।।२।।

[बिम्बोत्सेधाः।]

उक्तमार्गेण सर्वेषामन्योन्यविधि योज्यताम्[5] ।
बिम्बमानाद् गृहं कुर्याद् गृहमानाच्च बिम्बकृत् ।।३।।
द्विविधं[6] ग्राह्यमानन्तु[7] अन्यमानं न पूजितम् ।।३½।।

बिम्बमानप्रमाणेन[8] योजितं बिस्तृत [म्] आलये[9] ।
तेनैव बिम्बमानेन द्वारमाणन्तु तद्विधेत् ।।४।।

बिम्बस्य मानात्[10] त्रिगुणैव[11] तारम्
अर्धांशहीनं[12] द्विगुणं तथैव ।
अध्यर्धमानं[13] गृहबिम्बमानम्
एतानि[14] सम्यग्विधिवद्[15] विधिज्ञः[16] ।।५।।

---

१. अ. शृणुः । २. अ. निशण्ण॰ । ३. अ. ॰काष्टेस्टिका॰ । ४. अ. प्रवक्षते। ५. अ. ग. ॰योज्यकाम् । ६. ग. द्विधा । ७. अ. गृह्य मानन्तु । ग. ग्रयिहं माणन्तु। ज. द्विविधाग्राह्यमानात्तु । ८. अ. ॰प्रमानेन । ९. अ. योजितविस्त्रितालये । ग. विस्तितालयेत्। ज. योजिते विस्तृतालये ।१०. ग. बिम्बस्य मान । ११. अ. त्रिगुनैव । १२. ग. घर्धांशहीन। १३. अ. अर्धार्धमानं । ग. अद्यर्ध॰ । १४. ग. मेतानि । १५. अ. सम्यक्विधि॰। १६. ज. विधिज्ञैः ।

The Bimbamāna of the Gautamīyaśāstra

as heard by Śāriputra

[The Three kinds of Image]

1. Listen! I shall now describe the iconometric system [pertaining to the Buddha image]. One shall consider it (i.e., the image) to be the three kinds [namely], the sedent, the standing and the recumbent.

[Materials for making Images]

2. That image in whose construction one of such materials as gold, copper, clay, stone, wood, brick and stucco (lime) is used will now be described.

[Relative Measurements of Image-house and Principal Image]

3. In all cases, relative measurements as stated below may be applied; one shall construct the image-house to be proportionate to the height (lit., measurement) of the image and vice versa (i.e., the image to be proportionate to the measurement[1] of the image-house). The measurement acceptable are thus twofold. No other measurement recommended.
4. The width of the [image-] house is determined in relation to the height (lit., measurement) of the image. The measurement of the door [of the image-house] should likewise be made proportionate to the same measurement of the image.
5. The width [of the image-house may be] three times the height (lit., measurement) of the image, two and a half times, twice, and similarly one and a half times the height of the resident image. One who is conversant with the rules shall thus properly [carry out his work] as has been laid down [in the *śāstras*].

---

1. The width, which is considered the most important measurement in Oriental architecture.

विशालबिम्बस्य[१] गृहेऽपि तारम्
बिम्बोदयं[२] स्यात् सममेव शस्तम्[३] ।
अथापि ताराद्[४] द्विमुखञ्च[५] हीनं
तदर्धवक्त्रं गृहमेव युक्तम् ।।६।।

अथ ऊर्ध्वम्प्रवक्ष्यामि[६] मानाद् बिम्बेऽपि[७] भेदकम्[८] ।
हस्तद्वयमधः शेषम्[९] अल्पबिम्बम् प्रवक्ष्यते[१०] ।।७।।

तदूर्ध्वम्[११] पञ्चहस्तान्तम् बिम्बाधममिति स्मृतम् ।
पञ्चादि[१२] अष्टहस्तान्तम् मध्यमबिम्बमुच्यते[१३] ।।८।।

तदूर्ध्वम्[१४] द्वादशान्तञ्च उत्तमेति[१५] प्रकीर्तितम् ।
द्वादशादावशीत्यन्तम्[१६] महाबिम्बोच्यते[१७] क्रमात् ।।९।।

चलाचलम् प्रयुञ्जीयात्[१८] सर्वबिम्बं हितार्थकम्[१९] ।
स्वर्णादिलोहबिम्बे च देहगर्भन्न कारयेत्[२०] ।।१०।।

बिम्बं[२१] गर्भेण[२२] संयुक्तं कलत्रोपद्रवं[२३] कारयेत् ।
कलहो द्रव्यनाशञ्च[२४] न चिरात् क्षुद्भयं भवेत् ।।११।।

कर्मान्त श्चापि बाध्यन्ते राजानाम्[२५] प्रतिषेधनम्[२६] ।
काष्ठपाषाणबिम्बे[२७] च यत् सन्धौ विधिरुच्यते[२८] ।।१२।।

---

१. ग. विसाल° । २. ग. °दय । ३. अ. सस्तम् । ४. अ.क.ग. तारम् । ५. ग. मुखञ्च। ६. अ.क.ग. ऊर्धम् । क.ग. °प्रवक्षामि । ७. क.ग. बिम्बानि । ज. बिम्बानुभेदकम् । ८. क. भेदकात् । ग. भेदकां । ९. अ.क.ग. °मधोशेषाम् । १०. अ.क.ग. प्रवक्षते । ११. क. ग. तदुर्धम् । ज. तदूर्ध्वे । १२. ज. पञ्चादौ । १३. अ. °बिम्बमुच्चते । क. बिम्बवुच्चते। १४. क. तदु... । ग. तदुर्द्ध । ज. तदूर्ध्वे । १५. ग. उत्तमम् । १६. अ. द्वादशान्तावसी°। क. °हस्तावसी° । १७. क. °बिम्बोच्चते । ज. महाबिम्बं यथा क्रमात् । १८. ग. प्रयुञ्जिश्यात्। १९. ज. °बिम्बहितार्थकम् । २०. ग. °गर्ब्भण्णकारयेत् । २१. अ.क.ज. बिम्बात् । ग. बिम्बां। २२. अ.क. गर्भेन । २३. अ. कलतृपद्रव । क.ग. कलत्रपदव्यन्तु । ज. कलेवरन्तु। २४. अ. कलहोपद्रव्य° । ग. °नासञ्च । २५. अ. राज्ञानाम् । क. राज्ञानम् । ग. राजानम्। ज. राज्ञश्च । २६. अ. प्रतिशोधते । क. प्रतिसोधने । ग. प्रतिसेधते । २७. अ. काष्टपासान°। क.ग. काष्ट° । २८. क. विधिरुच्चते ।

6. Should the width of the [image-] house be equal to [the height of] the image which is large, it would also be commendable. And if the width is less [than the height of the image] two face-lengths[1] or half of a face-length, it would [still] suit the [image] house.

[Classification of Images according to Height].

7. I shall next enumerate the image types [determined] according to the height. All [images] which are below two *hastas* [in height] are called minor idols (*alpa-bimba*).

8. An image [with a height] from two to five *hastas* is said to belong to the *adhama* [variety] and that from five to eight *hastas* to the *madhyama* [variety].

9. [The image which is] above that the below twelve [*hastas*] is declared [to be of the] *uttama* [type]. [That image] between twelve *hastas* and eighty [*hastas*] is called in order the *mahābimba* (or grand image).

[Rule Governing Cast Images]

10. One shall make all images bestowing welfare either movable or immovable. One shall not make images made of metals such as gold with hollow inside.

11. The image with cavity inside shall spell disaster for the spouse; there shall also be strife, loss of wealth and fear of starvation near at hand.

12a. Work too will suffer [and there will be] repudiation of the rulers.

12b. The methods [to be followed] in the case of joints in images wrought out of wood or stone will [now] be stated.

---

1. The face-length is the vertical distance from the hair-limit to the end of the jaw or the horizontal measurement between the two ears in front. In certain *śilpa* texts, however, the vertical measurement is slightly less than the horizontal measurement. It is, therefore, advisable to take the horizontal measurement as the standard face-length.

सन्धि सन्धेन[१] कर्तव्यम् असन्धिकं[२] न गृह्यते[३] ।
एवमुक्तविधानेन आयुर्भोगन्तु वर्धनम् ।।१३।।
विपरीतेन संयुक्तं सर्वभोगायुनाशनम्[४] ।।१३½।।

सर्वेषां[५] गृह्यमाणन्तु[६] मात्रार्धेन[७] यवेन वा ।
तस्मान्नश्यति निर्दिष्टं हीनवृद्धिन्न[८] कारयेत् ।।१४।।

येन[९] बिम्बप्रमाणे[१०] च मानाङ्गुलविभाजिते[११] ।
तेन बिम्बस्य[१२] मानन्तु तत्र चायाममिष्यते[१३] ।।१५।।
यावद्वक्षःस्थले[१४] तारन् तारमेवन्तु[१५] गृह्यते[१६] ।।१५½।।

[योनिनक्षत्रादीनि ।]
इत्युक्तप्रमाणेन[१७] मानाङ्गुलेन सङ्गमम् ।
तस्मिन् उक्तैव[१८] मानन्तु योनिनक्षत्रसंयुतम्[१९] ।।१६।।

आयमष्टगुणिते[२०] च द्वादशांशे तु[२१] शेषता[२२] ।
नन्दांशे तु[२३] गुणितेऽपि धर्मांशे[२४] तु व्ययम्भवेत्[२५] ।।१७।।

योनिर्गुणैर्गुणिते[२६] च अष्टांशे ऽपि तथैव च ।
ऋक्षं चाष्टगुणिते[२७] च सप्तविंशतिशेषकः[२८] ।।१८।।

---

१. ज. सन्धिसन्धेन । २. अ. असन्धीक । क.ग. असन्धिकन्तु । ३. क. ग्रह्यते । ४. अ.क.ग. °नासनम् । ५. क.ग. सर्वेसाम् । ६. अ. गृयृह्मानन्तु । ७. क. मात्रार्धं । ज. मात्रार्धाद् वा । ८. ग. हीण उर्धन्न । ९. अ. यद् । क.ग. यत् । १०. अ. °प्रमानेन । ११. अ.क.ग. °विभाजितम् । १२. अ. बिम्बश्य । क. बिम्बेश्य । १३. अ. °मिश्यते । क. नतवायाममिश्यते । ग. नतुवायाम° । १४. अ. वक्ष्यस्थले । क.ग. वक्षस्थलम् । १५. अ.क.ग. कारमेवन्तु । १६. अ.क. ग्रयृह्ते । १७. अ. °प्रमानेन । १८. अ. तस्मिमुक्तेव । क. तस्मिं युक्ते च । १९. ग.ज. संयुक्तम् । २०. अ.क.ग. आयामष्टगुणितौ । ज. आयन्चाष्ट° । २१. अ. द्वादशांश तु । क. द्वादशांशति । ग. द्वादसांशेति । २२. क. शेषता । ग. सेसता । २३. अ. नन्दांसेति । क.ग. नन्दांशेति । २४. अ. धर्माङ्गे । २५. ग. व्यम्भ° । २६. अ. °गुणिर् गुणितौ । क. °गुणितौभिर्गुणितौ । ग. °गुणिभिर्गुणितौ । २७. अ.क.ग. ऋक्षकाष्टगुणितौ । २८. ग. सेसकः । ज. शेषता ।

13. The joints of images of wood and stone must be placed exactly where the joints are, and not otherwise. If images are made thus, it will result in length of days. If done in a contrary manner loss of life and all enjoyment [will follow].

[Importance of Accuracy of Measurement]

14. It is laid down that, in all cases, the measurements taken will perish on account of the measurements being out by half an *aṅgula* or [even] a *yava*. One should not, therefore, make the measurement shorter or longer [than it should be].

15. When the height (lit. measurement) of an image is divided by *mānāṅgulas*, that measurement of the image [thus obtained] is desired to be its length. Likewise the breadth of the chest is taken to be [its] width.

[The Six Kinds of Formula]

16. When the given measurement is taken in *mānāṅgulas*, the same measurement [shall be] in conformity with [the six formulas such as] *yoni, nakṣatra* etc.

17. When [the desired measurement is] multiplied by eight and [the result] divided by twelve the remainder is [called] *āya*; when [the desired measurement is] multiplied by nine and [the result divided] by ten [the remainder] shall be called *vyaya*.

18. When [the desired measurement] is multiplied by three [and divided] by eight [the remainder] is [called] *yoni*; when [the desired measurement] is multiplied by eight and [divided by] twenty-seven the remainder [shall be called] *ṛkṣa*.

वारं[१] नवगुणिते[२] च सप्तांशे तु हृतम्भवेत्[३] ।
अंशकञ्चाष्टगुणिते[४] (ऽपि) नवभागाधिकम्मतम्[५] ।।१९।।

तस्मात् सर्वेषु-म्-इत्युक्तं[६] विपरीतन्न कारयेत् ।
विपरीतेन[७] संयुक्तं[८] राजराष्ट्रविनाशनम्[९] ।।२०।।

स्थानभ्रंशं[१०] [च] आदेश्यं[११] चिरमायुर्न वर्धति ।
यजमानादिकधाम[१२] युक्तं कुर्याद् विचक्षणः[१३] ।।२१।।

[बिम्बानां देहमानम् ।]
अथ ऊर्ध्वम्[१४] प्रवक्ष्यामि[१५] बिम्बानां[१६] देहमानकम् ।
चतुर्विंशच्छतं[१७] श्रेष्ठदशतालोद्भवपर्वणा[१८] ।।२२।।

द्विकलार्धाङ्गुलम्भागन् त्रयोदशार्धाङ्गुलम्मुखम् ।
यावत् पादादिकेशान्तम् भागार्धन् नववक्त्रकम्[१९] ।।२३।।

वक्त्रमाणं त्रिभागं स्यात् सर्वमाणन्तु गृह्यते[२०] ।
यवाष्टकमुष्णीषश्च[२१] शिरोमाणं त्र्यङ्गुलम्[२२] ।।२४।।

केशान्तादक्षिसूत्रान्तात्[२३] पुटान्ताद्धनुमेव[२४] च ।
भागभागस्तथैवन्तु गलमर्धाङ्गुलम्मतम्[२५] ।।२५।।

---

१. अ.क.ग. वारकं । २. अ. °गुणितौ। क.ग. नवोगुणितौ । ३. अ. हृदयं भ° । ४. अ. अंशकं चाश्टगु° । क. अंशकाष्ट° । ज. अंशो द्व्यब्धिगु° । ५. क.ग. °धिकर्म्मतम् । ज. °धिको मतः । ६. अ. सवैरपि त्युक्तम् । क. सर्वेषुमित्तकम् । ग. सर्वेसुमित्तुक्तम् । ७. क.ग. विपरितानि । ८. ज. संयुक्ताद् । ९. अ. राजाराष्ट्रा विनासनम् । क. ग. °विनासनम् । १०. अ. ब्रींशम् । ग. भ्रिंशम् । ११. अ.ग. आदेसं । १२. अ. यजमानादी तद्ध्वामं । क. °दिकध्वामं । ग. यजमानादिद्धवामं । ज. °दितद्धामं । १३. अ. विचक्षनः । १४. अ. उध्वम् । क.ग. ऊर्धम् । १५. क.ग. प्रवक्षामि । १६. ग. बिम्बाणं । १७. अ. °विशतिसतस्रेष्टं । क. °विशतिशत । ग. °विशतिशतं । १८. क.ग. श्रेष्टम् दश° °पर्वकौ। अ. °पर्वकौ । १९. क. भागार्धनव° । ज. भागादिनव° । २०. अ. गृयृहते । २१. अ. °मुष्णिश्च। क. यद्वाष्टमुहुण्णिश्श्च । ग. यवाष्टमुण्णीशस्च । ज. यवाष्ट मूर्ध्नि उष्णीषः । २२. अ. क.ग. त्रयंगुलम् । २३. अ. °सूत्रान्त । क.ग. केशान्ताचक्षिसूत्रान्तात् । २४. क.ग. पुटान्ताहनु° । २५. क. गुलमंद्ध्यांगुल° । ग. गुलं मद्ध्यां° ।

19. When [the desired measurement] is multiplied by nine and divided by seven [the remainder] shall be called *vāra*; when [the desired measurement] is multiplied by eight and divided by nine, [the balance] left over is considered to be *aṃśa*.

20. One shall not, therefore, act in all cases in a manner contrary to what has been said above. [If] done in a contrary manner, the destruction of the ruler and the state [will follow].

21. It should be pointed out that the loss of place [will follow], and the life span will no longer increase. The wise one shall [thus] construct the dwelling place of the patron in the proper manner.

[The Uttama-daśa-tāla Measure]

22. I shall next describe the body measurements of [the Buddha] image. It shall consist of one hundred and twenty-four [dehalabdha] *aṅgulas* based on the superior ten-*tāla* system.

23. [A unit of measure consisting of] two *kalās* and a half *aṅgula* (i.e. 4½ *aṅgulas*) is [called] a *bhāga*, thirteen and a half *aṅgulas* a face-length. The total height from the feet to the hair-limit shall be nine face-lengths and half of a *bhāga* (i.e., 123¾ *aṅgulas*)[1].

24. A face-length shall be three *bhāgas*, which is accepted in all instances in iconometry. The *uṣṇīṣa*[2] shall be eight *yavas* and the measurement of the head [up to the hair-limit] three *aṅgulas*.

25. From the hair-limit [to the eyeline], from the eyeline to the nostril and from the nostril to the jaw [limit] it shall be one *bhāga* in each case. Similarly the *gala*[3] is said to the be one half of an *aṅgula*.

---

1. This is rough calculation. The exact height, however, consists of 124 *aṅgulas*.
2. The crown or protuberance on the head of the Buddha.
3. The fleshy part projecting beyond the chin.

हिक्कादग्रीवा[१] ऽऽर्धन्तु[२] तावद् हृदयावधि[३] ।
हृदयान्[४] नाभिमेढ्रान्त[५] तालात्तालान्तरम्भवेत्[६] ॥२६॥

तालद्वयायतश्[७] चोरुर्[८] जङ्घा चोरुसमा मता[९] ।
पादजानु द्विभागं स्यान्[१०] मूलमानम्प्रकीर्तितम्[११] ॥२७॥

सप्तविंशाङ्गुलायामम्[१२] बाहोरायामम्[१३] उच्यते[१४] ।
विंशतिश्चापि[१५] मात्रन्तु कूर्परान् मणिसन्धिश्च[१६] ॥२८॥
तलायामम्प्रयुञ्जीयाद्[१७] वक्त्रमाणन् तदुच्यते[१८] ॥२८½॥

पर्यन्तकेशमुष्णीषात्[१९] कलापञ्च समुन्नतिः[२०] ।
तावच्च[२१] पार्श्वदेशन्तु[२२] मानम्[२३] एकादशाङ्गुलम् ॥२९॥

पृष्ठं[२४] शीर्षस्य वक्त्रन्तु यावन्नाहन् त्रिवक्त्रयुक्[२५] ।
कर्णात्कर्णञ्च[२६] दीर्घन्तु कोलकैकादशांशयुक्[२७] ॥३०॥

तदन्तरम् पृष्ठमुखेन कुर्यात्
केशस्य पिण्डोपरिमाणमुक्तम् ।
यवत्रयोविंशति नाहमानम्[२८]
वृत्तित्रयन्[२९] दक्षिणवृत्तकेशम्[३०] ॥३१॥

---

१. ग. ज. ग्रीवान् । २. अ.क.ग. त्रयार्धन्तु । ३. अ. °यावधिः । ग. ह्रिदयान्तं । ज. हृदयावधिम् । ४. अ.क. हृदयान्तात् । ग. ह्रिदयान्तं । ज. हृदयान्तान् । ५. अ.क. ठ. °मेढ्रा च । ज. °मेढ्रञ्च । ६. अ. तालान्ताला° । ७. अ. तालद्वयायाम चोरु । क. °द्वयायतो । ग. °द्वयतो । ८. अ.क. चोरु । ग. ऊरु । ९. अ.क.ग. °समं मतम् । १०. क.ग. स्यात् । ११. ग. मूलमाणं । १२. ग. °विंशांगुलं यामं । १३. अ. बाहुरायामम् । क. °बाहुणामम् । १४. क.ग. उच्चते । १५. क. विंशतियवमात्र° । ग. विंशतिश्च । १६. अ. सन्धिषु । क.ग. °सन्धिसु । ज. °सन्धिञ्च । १७. अ. तलयाम प्रयुञ्जी° । १८. क. तदुच्चते । ग. °णमुच्चती । १९. अ. पर्यान्तं केश° । ग. पर्यान्तकेसमुष्णीशां । २०. अ.क. °समुन्नतिम् । ग. °समुण्णति । २१. अ.क.ग. तावत् । २२. ग. पाशदिसन्तु । २३. ज. मानाद् । २४. अ.क. पृष्टात् । २५. अ.क. °वक्त्रयुः । २६. अ. °कर्णौ च । २७. अ. °दशङ्गयुः । क. कोलकादशनाह्युः । ज. °दशन्तया । २८. अ. नागमानम् । २९. अ.क. वृतित्रयं । ३०. क. °केशाम् ।

26. [The height of] the neck from the hiccup [shall be] three and a half *aṅgulas*; from that point (i.e., the hiccup) to the chest-limit, from the chest-limit up to the navel and from the navel to [the root of] the generative organ it shall be one *tāla*[1].

27. The thigh shall be two *tālas* long and the shank is taken to be equal to the thigh [in length]. The foot and the knee shall be two *bhāgas*. The basic measurements [are thus] stated.

28. The length of the arm is said to be twenty-seven *aṅgulas* [long]. [The length of the hand] from the elbow to the wrist shall be twenty plus one *aṅgula*. One shall fix the length of the palm to be one face-length (i.e., 13½ *aṅgulas*).

29. The distance (lit., the height) from the *uṣṇīṣa* to the hair-limit [in front shall be] five *kalās* (i.e., ten *aṅgulas*). The measurement from the same [to the hair-limit] on the sides [shall be] eleven *aṅgulas*.

30. [The measurement of] the back of the head [shall be] one face-length and its circumference three face-lengths[2]. The distance (lit., length) between the two ears in front shall likewise be eleven *kolakas* (i.e., twenty-two *aṅgulas*).

31. One shall make the interval [between the two ears] at the back one face-length (i.e., thirteen and a half *aṅgulas*)[3]. The measurement [of each] knob of hair [on the head] is stated [as follows]: the circumference is twenty-three *yavas*; its hair has curled inwards thrice in clọckwise direction.

---

1. Here and also in the following verses '*tāla*' stands for a face-length of 13½ *aṅgulas* and not 12 *aṅgulas*.

2. Here the face-length should be taken as a *tāla* (of 12 *aṅgulas*) and not 13½ *aṅgulas*.

3. This would mean that half an *aṅgula* is left out for the station of the two ears. The *Citrakarmaśāstra* leaves one *aṅgula* for the two ears (xiv.10).

विस्ताराष्टयवं[1] विद्यात् षड्यवन्[2] तुङ्गमिष्यते[3] ।
सवेदत्रिमुखं नाहम्[4] अर्कश्शरशतत्रयम्[5] ।।३२।।

कलापञ्च ललाट[6] स्यात्[7] कर्णान्ताद्[8] वक्त्रमाणकम् ।
एकादश[9] कपोलाग्र[10] दश[11] चिबुकमानकम्[12] ।।३३।।
अधरान्ते (च) नवाङ्गुलं[13] हनुचक्रञ्च[14] भागयुक्[15] ।।३३½।।

ग्रीवामूलन्नवाङ्गुल्यम् अग्रमष्टाङ्गुलम्भवेत् ।
बाहुमूलन्नवाङ्गुल्यम् प्रकोष्ठमूलं (तु) सप्तकम्[16] ।।३४।।

कूर्परन्तु[17] षडङ्गुल्यम्[18] मणिसन्धि[19] [तु] त्र्यर्धकम्[20] ।
तलतारं[21] षडङ्गुल्यन्[22] तावदायामं[23] सप्तकम् ।।३५।।

चत्वारिंशांगुलार्धञ्च बाहुविस्तारमिष्यते[24] ।
द्वाविंशत्यङ्गुलार्धञ्च[25] कक्षयोरन्तरम्भवेत् ।।३६।।

स्तनान्ताद्[26] ऊनविंशच्च[27] मध्यमं[28] चाष्टकोलकम् ।
नवकोलकमात्रन्तु मेढ्रमूलन्तद्[29] उच्यते[30] ।।३७।।

---

१. क. विस्तारस्टयवं । २. अ.क.ग. षट्यवं । ३. अ. °मिश्यते । ४. अ. नागं । ५. अ. मर्कष्य च शत° । क.ग. मर्क्कश्यरशतं । ६. क. ललाट । ७. क. श्यात् । ८. अ. कर्ण्णान्तां । क. कर्ण्णान्ता । ग. कर्ण्णात् । ९. अ. एकादशाङ् । ग. दशाम् । १०. ग. कपोतञ्च । ११. अ.क. दशांगुलम् । ग. दसगुलम् । १२. क.ग. चुबुक° । अ. दशांगुलं चुबुकम्भवेत् । ज. चिबुकञ्च दशांगुलम् । १३. अ. नवांगुल्यधरान्ते च । क. नधरन्तञ्च । ग. णवांगुलम् धरन्ते च । १४. ग. हनुचक्त्रञ्च । १५. अ.क.ग. भागयुः । १६. ज. प्रकोष्ठो ऽङ्गुलसप्तकम् । ग. °सत्तकम् । १७. ज. कूर्प्परस्तु । १८. अ.क. षडांगुल्यम् । ग. सटांगुल्म् । १९. ग. मनिसन्धि । ज. °सन्धिस् । २०. अ.क.ग. त्रयार्धकम् । २१. अ.क.ग. तलातार । ज. तलं तार° । २२. अ.क. षडाङ्गुल्यम् । ग. सडांगुलम् । २३. अ.क.ग.ज. तावदायामसप्त° । २४. ग. °मिश्यते । २५. क.ग. द्वाविंशांगुला° । २६. क. स्तानान्तात् । ग. स्थानान्तं । २७. अ. °विंशा च । क. °विंशाश्च । २८. क. मद्ध्यमात् । २९. ग. मेढ्रमूलन्तु । ३०. क.ग. उच्चते ।

32. One shall know it to measure eight *yavas* across, and it is desired that its height be six *yavas*. The circumference [of the area covered by the knobs] shall be three faces plus one *bhāga*. [The total number of such hair knobs on the head be] three hundred and sixty.

33. The forehead shall be five *kalās* (i.e., ten *aṅgulas*) [long], [and the horizontal measurement] between the two ears one face-length. [The distance between] the two cheeks shall be eleven *aṅgulas* and the length of the chin (*cibuka*) ten *aṅgulas*. [The distance between] the extremities of the lower lip shall be nine *aṅgulas* and the *hanucakra* (jaw-circle) two *bhāgas* (i.e., eight *aṅgulas*).

34. The base of the neck shall be nine *aṅgulas* [wide] and its top eight *aṅgulas* [wide]. [The width of] the root of the arm shall be nine *aṅgulas* [and] the root of the hand (*prakoṣṭha*) seven *aṅgulas*.

35. [The width of] the elbow shall be six *aṅgulas* [and that of] the wrist three and a half [*aṅgulas*]. The width of the palm [shall be] six *aṅgulas* and its length seven [*aṅgulas*].

36. It is desired that the width of the shoulders be forty and a half *aṅgulas*. The distance between the two armpits shall be twenty-two and a half *aṅgulas*.

37. [The width at] the breast-limit [shall be] nineteen *aṅgulas* and the mid-[belly] eight *kolakas* (i.e., sixteen *aṅgulas*). It is said that [the width at] the root of the generative organ is nine *kolakas* and one *mātra* (i.e., nineteen *aṅgulas*).

ऊरुमूलन्तु वक्त्रञ्च जानु भागद्वयम्भवेत् ।
जङ्घा [स्यात्] सप्तमात्रन्तु[1] नलका भागमेव च ।।३८।।
तलतार[2] षडङ्गुल्यम् पार्ष्णिर्भागन्तथैव[3] च ।।३८½।।

सूत्राल्ललाटपर्यन्तमङ्गुलोपरिमाणकम्[4] ।
तावद्दीर्घन्तु[5] भागं स्यात् सूत्रमध्ये चतुर्यवम् ।।३९।।

समन्ताच्चापवद्वक्रा[6] केशान्ते तोरणाकृतिः[7] ।
भ्रूतलमङ्गुलञ्चैव[8] पृथुलन्द्वियवम्भवेत्[9] ।।४०।।

शराङ्गुलन्तदायामम्[10] भ्रूतलं[11] धनुराकृतिः ।
त्र्यङ्गुलम्भ्रुवोर्मध्ये द्वयङ्गुलञ्च भ्रुवन्तकम्[12] ।।४१।।

नेत्रं त्र्यङ्गुलायामं[13] करवीर-म्-उपाङ्गयुक्[14] ।
तत्तारं षड्यवमानं[15] द्वियवञ्चर्मयुग्मकम्[16] ।।४२।।

नेत्रायामन् त्रिभागं[17] स्यात् श्वेतभागं[18] द्विभागयुक्[19] ।
एकेन कृष्णभागेन दृष्टिर्यूका[20] प्रमाणतः[21] ।।४३।।

नेत्रान्तरं[22] कला (ञ्) चैव[23] मूलनासाङ्गुलोन्नता[24] ।
चर्मपृष्ठार्धमात्रेण[25] तावद् भ्रुवोन्नतं[26] वरम् ।।४४।।

---

१. अ. जङ्घात् शप्तमात्रन्तु । ज. जङ्घायोस् सप्त॰ । २. अ. तलातार । क. तलातारम्। ग. तलाकरम् । ज. तलन् तारषड्॰ । ३. अ.ग. पार्ष्णि॰। क. पार्ष्णीम् । ४. क.ग. ॰मङ्गुलोत्परि॰ । ५. अ.क. तावदीर्घ । ग. तावत् दीर्घ । ६. क.ग. वक्रम् । ७. अ.क.ग. ॰कृति । ८. अ. भ्रूतलावङ्गुल॰ । क.ग. भ्रूतलं मङ्गुल॰ । ९. अ.ग. पृथुलद्वि॰। १०. अ. चतुरङ्गुलम् । क. चराङ्गुलम् । ११. अ. भ्रूतलौ । क. भ्रूतलत् । १२. अ.क. भ्रूवान्तकम्। १३. अ. नेत्रत्रयाङ्गु॰ । क. नेत्रायतं । ग. नेत्रं त्रंगुलायामम् । १४. क.ग. करवीराण्यपाङ्गयुः। १५. अ. षट्यवामानम् । ग. षट्यवं मानम् । ज. षड्यवम् मानाद् । १६. क. द्वयवं॰ । १७. क. तत् त्रिभागं । १८. अ. श्वेतभागा । क. श्वेतभागं। १९. क. द्विभागयोः । २०. अ. दृष्टि । क.ग. द्रिष्टि । २१. अ. प्रमाणकः । २२. अ.क. नेत्रान्तर । २३. अ.क.ग.ज. कलाञ्चैव । २४. अ.क.ग. ॰ङ्गुलोन्नतिम् । २५. अ. चर्मदृष्टा । क.ग. चर्म्मद्रिष्टि । २६. अ.क.ग. भ्रुवोन्नतिम्।

38. The root of the thigh shall be one face-length (i.e., 13½ *aṅgulas*) and the knee two *bhāgas* (i.e., nine *aṅgulas*). The shank [shall be] seven *aṅgulas*, the ankle one *bhāga*, the width of the foot six *aṅgulas* and, similarly, the heel one *bhāga*.

39. The projection from the [*pārśva*]-*sūtra* to the end of the forehead shall be one *aṅgula*, its length one *bhāga* and [the interval between] the middle of the *sūtra* [and the forehead level] four *yavas*.

40. [The forehead] is curved all along like a bow and at the hair-limit it is shaped like an arch. The region of the eyebrow shall be one *aṅgula* [wide] and the width [of the eye-brow] two *yavas*.

41. The eyebrow is shaped like a bow; it is five *aṅgulas* long, its middle occupying three *aṅgulas* and its end two *aṅgulas*.

42. The eye extending from the inner corner to its outer corner (i.e., unguent spot) is three *aṅgulas* long; its width measures six *yavas* and its two skins (i.e., eyelids) two *yavas*.[1]

43. The length of the eye shall consist of three divisions; the white portion shall occupy two parts and the black portion one part. The pupil of the eye [shall be] one *yūkā*[2] in thickness.

44. The interval between the two eyes is one *kalā*; the height of the root of the nose is one *aṅgula*, the skin of the eyelid half an *aṅgula* and the elevation of the eye-brow is said to be equal [to it].

---

1. Each eye-lid one *yava* thick.
2. One-eighth part of a *yava*.

पुटद्वयायतञ्चैव[१] कला (ञ्)[२] चैकाङ्गुलम्भवेत् ।
अङ्गुलन्तु पुटोत्सेधं सुषिर (युस्)। तारं षड्यवम्[३] ।।४५।।

तावत्समं विशालञ्च[४] गोजीदण्ड[५] यवत्रयम् ।
पुटसूत्रान्नासिकालम्बं यवत्रयं[६] विधीयते ।।४६।।

हास्यभागान्तरं[७] वक्त्रं नेत्रभागान्तरं भ्रुवम ।
षड्यवोत्तुङ्गमेवं स्यात्[८] त्रिवङ्कञ्चोत्तरोष्ठकम्[९] ।।४७।।

हास्यम्भागायतञ्चैव[१०] उत्तरोष्ठार्धमात्रकम्[११] ।
तारमेवम्प्रयुञ्जीयात्[१२] पालिका यवतारयुक्[१३] ।।४८।।

अर्धाधिककलायामम्[१४] ओष्ठम्मात्रैव[१५] विस्तृतम्[१६] ।
हास्याधश्चिबुकमानं[१७] कोलकञ्च प्रकीर्तितम् ।।४९।।

सर्वावयवसंयुक्तं वदनं वृत्ताङ्गशोभनम्[१८] ।
नयनं विशालं[१९] कर्णं[२०] च दीर्घम्पञ्चकोलकम् ।।५०।।
नयनद्वयं[२१] मूलं स्यान् नालदीर्घन्त्रिकोलकम्[२२] ।।५०½।।

---

१. अ. °द्वयायामञ्चैव । २. ज. कलां । ३. अ. सुसिरयुस्तार । क. षट्यवं सुसिरुकारयुः । ज. षड्यवं शुशितारयुक् । ४. क.ग. तावत् विशालसमञ्चैव । ५. क.ग. गोजीदण्ड । ६. अ. यवत्रय । ७. अ. हाश्यभागा° । क. भागभागान्तरं । ८. अ. °मेवस्यां । ९. अ. °त्तरोष्टकं। क. चोष्टरोष्टकम् । ग. चोष्टरोष्टका । १०. अ. हाश्यभागा° । ११. अ. उत्ररोष्टार्ध° । क.ग. उत्तरोष्टा° । १२. अ. प्रयुञ्जिस्यात् । क. प्रयुञ्जिश्यात्। १३. अ. तारयुर्यवपालिका। क.ग. °तारयुः ।१४. अ. अर्धाधिकं कला°। १५. अ. ओष्टम्मात्रेव। क.ग. ओष्टमात्रेव । १६. क.ग. विस्त्रितम् । १७. अ. हास्यादधश्चुबक° । क. हास्याधश्यात् चुबुक° । ग. हास्यात् चुबुकमानन्तु । १८. अ. मुखमुत्तुङ्ग° । क. उत्ताङ्ग° । ग. उत्ताङ्ग° । १९. क.ग.ज. विशल° । २०. अ. कर्ण्णौ । ग.ज. कर्ण्णौ च । २१. अ.क.ग. नयनद्वय । ज. °द्वयन्तु । २२. क. नालदीर्घ ।

45. The length of the two nostrils shall be one *kalā* and one *aṅgula*, their height one *aṅgula*, and the breadth of the hole six *yavas*.

46. The width of the *gojīdaṇḍa*[1] [shall be] three *yavas* and [its height] equal to it. The protrusion of the nose below the *puṭasūtra*[2] [shall also be] three *yavas*.

47. The face lying between the two cheek regions and the brow lying between the two eye regions measure six *yavas* in elevation. The upper lip [has] three curves.

48. The mouth shall be one *bhāga*[3] long, and one shall enjoin the width of the upper lip to be half an *aṅgula*; the margin of the lip [shall occupy] two *yavas* (each *pālikā* being one *yava* wide).

49. The [lower] lip [shall be] two and a half *aṅgulas* and its width one *aṅgula*. The height (lit., measurement) of the chin below the mouth is declared to be one *kolaka*.

50. The face endowed with all [essential] features would look beautiful with round surface. The ears are two *aṅgulas* broad and five *kolakas* long. The upper ear shall be four *aṅgulas* and the length of the tube three *kolakas*.

---

1. The bridge-like portion between the nose-tip and the upper lip.
2. The horizontal line drawn in line with the lower limit of the nostrils. The tip of the nose hangs below this line.
3. 4½ *aṅgulas*.

नालतारार्धमात्रञ्च[१] तावद् द्वि-र्-अन्तरं समम्[२] ।
कर्णस्य[३] अग्रनालन्तु ग्रीवान्तात्तद् द्वि-र्-अन्तरम्[४] ।।५१।।
अध्यर्धाङ्गुलं[५] चैवं[६] कर्णपृष्ठोन्नतं[७] तु तत् ।।५१½।।

गलरेखार्धचन्द्रा[८] स्यात् कण्ठदीर्घं[९] त्र्यर्धकम् ।
हिक्कासूत्रार्धमात्रन्तु[१०] कण्ठमूलं[११] त्र्यङ्गुलम्[१२] ।।५२।।

कक्षसन्धि द्वि-र-अङ्गुल्यं[१३] हिक्कासूत्रस्य मानकम् ।
हिक्कासूत्रादधः कक्षमानम्भागद्वयम्भवेत्[१४] ।।५३।।

हिक्कात्स्तनान्तरं स्यात्[१५] त्रयोदशार्धाङ्गुलम्मतम्[१६] ।
स्तनपीठस्तनाकारं[१७] षड्यवन्तुङ्गमेव च ।।५४।।

बाहुदीर्घं[१८] द्वितालञ्च[१९] सवक्त्रार्धम्[२०] प्रकोष्ठकम्[२१] ।
हिक्कात्कक्षान्तरन्[२२] तालमवलम्बन्तु[२३] कोलकम् ।।५५।।

तलतारं[२४] षडङ्गुल्यन्[२५] तत्र चायामं[२६] सप्तकम् ।
कोलकन्तु[२७] तलपार्श्वम्[२८] अध्यर्धमङ्गुष्ठतारता[२९] ।।५६।।

---

१. अ. नलतालार्धमात्राणि । क.ग. नलकारार्धमात्राणि। ज. °मात्रेण । २. क.ग. वद्यान्तरं समं । ३. क. कर्ण्णश्यात् अग्र° । ग. कर्ण्णश्याग्रणले। ४. अ. ग्रीवान्ताद्वि° । क. ग्रीवान्तदधिरन्त° । ग. ग्रीवान्तं वान्तु द्वरन्त° । ५. अ.ग. अर्धार्धाङ्गुलं । क. अर्धाङ्गुलं । ६. अ. चेव । ७. अ. पृष्टोन्नतिना । क. प्रिष्टोतान्तु । ग. प्रिष्टोन्तुनन् । ८. अ. °र्धचन्द्रनस्यात्। क. °चन्द्र । ग. °चन्द्रं । ९. क.ग. कण्ठदीर्घ । ज. कण्ठनीव्रन् । १०. ज. °सूत्रोर्ध्वमानन्तु। ११. क. कण्ठमूल । ज. स्कन्धमूलन् । १२. ग. त्रयार्धकम् । १३. क. द्विरङ्गुलम्। १४. क.ग. कक्षमान १५. अ. °स्तनान्तस्य । क.ग. °स्तनान्तरान्तश्य । १६. अ. त्रीदशार्धाङ्गु° । १७. अ. स्तानपीटस्तानकारम् । ग. स्थाणपिटस्तांकारं° । १८. अ. बाहुदीर्घा । १९. अ.क.ग. द्वितालानि । २०. क. वक्त्राद्यर्ध । ग. वक्त्राद्यं । २१. अ.क.ग. प्रकोष्टकम् । २२. अ. °कक्षान्तरञ्चापि । २३. क. कालं मवलम्बन्तु । अ. तालं लबन्तु । २४. अ. तलातार। क. स्तलतारा। ग. नालकार। २५. क.ग. सडाङ्गुल्यम्। ज. षडाङ्गुल्यन्। २६. अ.क.ग.ज. तत्र चायाम°। २७. अ. कोलकन्तल°। २८. ग. तलापार्श्व। २९. अ. तदर्धाङ्गुष्टतारकम् । क.ग. द्यर्धाङ्गुष्टतारतत्। ज. द्वयर्धाङ्गुष्ठ°।

51. The width of the tube of the ear [shall be] half an *aṅgula* and its either end equal in width. The interval between the lobe of the ear and the outer limit of the neck [shall be] one and a half *aṅgula*. Such is the elevation of the outer ear.

52. The *gala-rekhā* shall be crescent-shaped and the height (lit., length) of the neck three and a half [*aṅgulas*]. [Of this] half an *aṅgula* [will be taken up by] the hiccup-line. The distance from above the hiccup-line to the base of the neck [shall be] three *aṅgulas*.

53. The *kakṣa-sandhi* (armpit joint) shall be two *aṅgulas* from the hiccup-line. The armpit shall be two *bhāgas* (i.e., eight *aṅgulas*) below the hiccup-line[1].

54. The distance from the hiccup-line to each breast is said to be thirteen and a half *aṅgulas*. The seat of the breasts [shall be] six *yavas* high.

55. The length of the arm [shall be] two *tālas* (i.e., twenty-seven *aṅgulas*) and the fore-arm one and a half face-length[2]. The distance from the hiccup to the armpit [shall be] one *tāla* and the protrusion of the armpit one *kolaka*.

56. The width of the palm [shall be] six *aṅgulas* and its length seven [*aṅgulas*]. The side of the palm[3] [shall measure] one *kolaka* and the width of the thumb one and a half *aṅgula*.

---

1. This is the vertical distance between the hiccup-line and the armpit. According to the *Citrakarmaśāstra*, the distance from there to the breast-line is 5½ *aṅgulas* (xiv.33). This would make the distance between the hiccup-line and the breast-line 13½ *aṅgulas*.

2. This would make the length of the fore-arm 20¼ *aṅgulas*. The exact length is , however, 21 *aṅgulas*. See Verse 28 above.

3. That is, the thickness of the palm.

चतुर्यवाधिकषण्मात्रं[१] मध्यमाङ्गुलिदीर्घता[२] ।
पञ्चाङ्गुलार्धानामिका[३] (च) यवहीना[४] प्रदेशिनी ।।५७।।

द्विकोलकन्[५] द्वियवाधिक्यं[६] कनिष्ठाङ्गुलिदीर्घता[७] ।
मध्यमाङ्गुलितारन्तु यवाध्यङ्गुलमेव च[८] ।।५८।।

अङ्गुलन्तु सविस्तारे[९] ऽनामिका च प्रदेशिनी[१०] ।
कनिष्ठा[११] षड्यवन्तारा[१२] मूलाङ्गुष्ठो ऽध्यर्धकम्[१३] ।।५९।।

अङ्गुष्ठस्य द्विपर्वणी[१४] अङ्गुलनखविस्तृतम्[१५] ।
मध्यमाङ्गुलिनखतारं[१६] षड्यवं विधिवत् कुरु[१७] ।।६०।।

तर्जन्यनामिके[१८] तस्य[१९] यवपञ्च[२०] विशालकम् ।
कनिष्ठाङ्गुलिनखतारं[२१] यवत्रयं[२२] विधीयते ।।६१।।

अक्षात्पादतलायामन् त्रयोदशार्धाङ्गुलम्भवेत्[२३] ।
नलकायामं[२४] भागं[२५] स्यात् तारमेतत्प्रयोजयेत्[२६] ।।६२।।

---

१. ज. °षण्मात्रा । २. अ. °दीर्गतत् । क.ग. °दीर्घतत् । ३. क. °ङ्गुलार्धनामिका । ग. °ङ्गुलानामिका च । ज. °ङ्गुलार्द्धम् अनामी च । ४. अ. यवहीनम् । क.ग. यवहीनं । ५. अ.क.ग. द्विकोलकञ्च । ज. द्विकोलकद्वि° । ६. अ. साधिक्य । क. यवाधिक्यं । ग. यवाधिकं । ७. अ.क. °ङ्गुष्टदीर्घतत् । ग. °ङ्गुलिदीर्ग्घतत् । ज. °ङ्गुष्ठदीर्ग्घ° । ८. अ. यवाधिक्यांगुलिन्तथा । क. यवाधिकाङ्गुलि° । ९. अ.क. सविस्तारम् । ग. विस्तारं । १०. अ.ग. प्रदेशनी । ११. अ. कणिष्ठाण् । १२. अ. षड्यवन्तारम् । ग. कनिष्टसत्यवविस्तारं । १३. क. मूलङ्गुष्टतद्यर्धकम् । अ. मूलाङ्गुष्टार्धकम्मतम् । ग. मूलाङ्गुष्टविद्याधकं । ज. °ङ्गुष्ठो द्वयर्धकम् । १४. अ.क.ग. द्विपर्वाणि । ग. द्विपाश्वानि । १५. क. नखविभक्तिर्तं । ग. विस्त्रिकं । १६. ग. मूलमाङ्गुल्य° । अ.क. °नखातारम् । ज. °माङ्गुल्यनखा° । १७. अ.क.ग. गुरुः । १८. अ.क.ग. °नामिका । १९. ज. तयोर् । अ. तस्स । क.ग. तश्य । २०. क. यवा पञ्च । २१. अ.क. °नखातारम् । ज. कन्याङ्गुल्यनखा । २२. अ.ग. यवत्रय । २३. अ. त्रोदशार्धाङ्गुल° । २४. अ.क.ज. नलकायाम । ग. नलकायम । २५. ज. भागा । २६. क.ग. °प्रणीजयेत् ।

57. The length of the middle finger [shall be] six *aṅgulas* and four *yavas*, the ring-finger five and a half *aṅgulas* [long] and the index finger one *yava* less [than the former].

58. The length of the little finger [shall measure] two *kolakas* and two *yavas*. The width of the middle finger [shall be] one *aṅgula* and one *yava*.

59. The ring-finger and the index finger [shall measure] one *aṅgula* in width [while] the little finger [shall be] six *yavas* wide and the thumb is said to be one and a half *aṅgulas* [wide].

60. The thumb has two links; the width of its nail [shall be] one *aṅgula*. Make as enjoined the middle-finger-nail six *yavas* wide.

61. The width of those (i.e., of the nails) of the index and ring fingers [shall be] five *yavas* [each]. It is enjoined that the width of the little-finger-nail be three *yavas*.

62. The length of the foot from the ankle shall be thirteen and a half *aṅgulas*, and the length of the *nalakā* one *bhāga*[1]. One shall employ its width as follows.

---

1. 4½ *aṅgulas*.

तारं द्विमात्रकञ्चैव[१] तुर्यवाधिकभागिकम्[२] ।
पादाङ्गुष्ठस्तु[३] एवं स्यात् पादः[४] षड्यवोन्नतिः[५] ।।६३।।

अश्विन्यङ्गुलिदीर्घञ्च[६] त्रिमात्रार्धाङ्गुलम्भवेत् ।
एतत्पादाङ्गुलाञ्चैव[७] अर्धमर्धम्प्रशून्यता[८] ।।६४।।

ईशावतारभानुश्च मार्गधर्मर्तुस्[९] तत्क्रमात्[१०] ।
पञ्चाङ्गुलततिर्ज्ञेया[११] मार्गतारन्तथैव[१२] च ।।६५।।

अङ्गुष्ठस्य[१३] नखायामं सयवाङ्गुलमिष्यते[१४] ।
तत्तारं यवहीनं[१५] स्यान्मांसोपरि[१६] यवार्धकम् ।।६६।।

पृष्ठकक्षान्तरन्तारं[१७] वक्त्रद्वयं[१८] विधीयते ।
मध्यमाष्टकला ज्ञेया[१९] श्रोणितारं कला नव[२०] ।।६७।।
दशकलाश्च[२१] विज्ञेयं[२२] जघनस्थलं[२३] विधीयते ।।६७½।।

पृष्ठमष्टाङ्गुलञ्चैव[२४] तावदुन्नतं[२५] कोलकम् ।
ऊरुमूलान्तरं मात्रं[२६] जानुद्व्यन्तरं[२७] कोलकम् ।।६८।।
अक्षद्व्यन्तरं[२८] भागं स्यात्[२९] पादाङ्गुष्ठं[३०] कलाधिकम् ।।६८½।।

---

१. अ. तारद्विमात्र° । क.ग. °मात्रक° । ज. तारद्विमात्रकम्चैव । २. ज. चतुर्य्यवा° । ३. अ. °ङ्गुष्टस्य । क.ग. पादाङ्गुष्ट° । ज. पादाङ्गुष्ठ । ४. अ. पदे । क.ग. पादं । ५. अ. षड्यवमुन्नतिम् । क.ग. षड्यवोन्नतिम् । ६. अ. अश्विन्याङ्गुलि° । ७. अ. तत्पादाङ्गुलाश्चैव । क. तत्पादाङ्गुलिञ्चैव । ज. °ङ्गुलाञ्चैव । ८. अ. अर्धमद्रप्रसून्यताम् । क. अर्धमर्धप्रगुण्यताम् । ज. अर्धमर्धप्र° । ९. अ. धर्मतु । क. °धम्मार्द्रितु° । ग. धर्म्मत्रृतु । १०. क.ग.ज. क्रमात् । ११. अ.क. ततिज्ञेयम् । ग. °ततिज्ञेय्य । ज. °ङ्गुलितति° । १२. अ. एवमानन्तथैव । १३. अ. अङ्गुष्टस्य । क. अङ्गुष्टश्य । ग. अङ्गुष्टनखा° । १४. अ. क.ग. °मिश्यते । १५. क.ग. °हीनश्यात् । १६. अ. मन्शोपरि° । क.ग. मासोपरि° । १७. अ.क.ग. पृष्ट° । १८. अ.क.ग. वक्त्रद्वय । १९. अ. ज्ञेयम् । क.ज. ज्ञेय्या । २०. क.ग. नवा कला । २१. अ. कला च दश । २२. अ. विज्ञेय । ग. विज्ञेय्यम् । ज. विज्ञेय्या । २३. अ. जङ्घास्यल । क. °स्थल । ग. जगनस्थल । ज. जङ्घास्थला । २४. अ. पृष्टाङ्गुल° । क.ग. पृष्टमष्टा° । २५. अ.क.ग.ज. उन्नत° । २६. ज. मात्रां । २७. अ. जानुद्वान्तर । क. जानुद्वन्त्र । ग. जान्वन्तर । ज. जान्वोर् अन्तर° । २८. अ. अक्षद्वान्तर । क. अक्षात् द्वेसन्तार । ग. अक्षद्वौतार । ज. अक्षद्वयान्तर° । २९. अ. स्या । ३०. अ. पोदाङ्गुष्ट । क.ग. पादाङ्गुष्ट ।

63. The width [shall be] two *aṅgulas* and [the length] of the big toe one *bhāga* and four *yavas*.[1] The height of the foot [shall be] six *yavas*.

64. The length of the second toe shall be three and a half *aṅgulas*. The remaining toes shall decrease [in length successively] by one half [in each case].

65. Sixteen, twelve, ten, eight and six [*yavas*]—the widths of the five toes should be known to be as such in the same order. The [length and] breadth of the ten [toes] were thus [given].

66. It is desired that the length of the nail of the big toe be one *aṅgula* and one *yava*; its width shall be one *yava* less [than an *aṅgula*] and the fleshy part round the nail half a *yava* [wide].

67. The distance between the two armpits at the back is enjoined as two face-lengths (i.e., 27 *aṅgulas*); the belly should be known to be eight *kalās*, the width of the hip and the lions nine *kalās* and the [the width of] the buttocks ten *kalās*.

68. [The generative organ shall measure] eight *aṅgulas* from outside and its height one *kolaka*. The interval between the roots of the [two] thighs shall be one *aṅgulas*, and that between the two knees one *kolaka*, that between the two ankles one *bhāga*,[2] and that between the two big toes one *kalā* more (i.e., 6½ *aṅgulas*).

---

1. Here *bhāga* should be taken as four *aṅgulas* because the big toe cannot be longer than five *aṅgulas*. According to other *śilpa* texts the length of the big toe lies between four *aṅgulas* plus two *yavas* and four *aṅgulas* plus four *yavas*.
2. 4½ *aṅgulas*.

[लम्बमानविधानम् ।]

मूर्ध्निमध्ये[१] च नासाग्रे[२] हृदये योनिनाभिके[३] ।
पादमध्ये[४] च जान्वोश्च[५] लम्बयेद् मध्यसूत्रकम् ।।६९।।

पिप्पली[६]मूर्ध्निबाह्ये[७] च बाहुपार्श्वे च मण्डले ।
जानुगुल्फोरुमध्ये[८] तु लम्बयेत् पार्श्वसूत्रकम् ।।७०।।

देशे देशे[९] प्रमाणन्तु[१०] त्रिगुणन्नाहमानतः ।
चीवरधरहस्तन्तु[११] बाहुतत्समतुङ्गकः ।।७१।।

अभयहस्तन्तु तन्मानं हनुहास्यपुटसीमकम् ।
मुखबाह्यात्स्तनाक्षाच्च[१२] नीत्वा च यवमष्टकम्[१३] ।।७२।।

कनिष्ठाङ्गुलिपार्श्वे च कटिमध्ये चोरुमध्यतः[१४] ।
तथैव जानुबाह्ये[१५] च लम्बयेत् कटिसूत्रकम् ।।७३।।

कर्णपार्श्वेन[१६] नीत्वा तु[१७] कोलकत्रयमेव च ।
कक्षबाह्ये त्र्यङ्गुल्यम्[१८] ऊर्ध्वबाहोस्तथैव[१९] च ।।७४।।

एतेन[२०] सूत्रमाणेनाभयहस्तन्तु कल्पितम् ।
कटका(भया)ङ्गुष्ठमन्तर्यं[२१] विंशद्व्यङ्गुलमुच्यते[२२] ।।७५।।

---

१. अ. मूर्धनिमध्यम । क.ग. मुह्णुर्ण्णि° । २. क. नाश्र्याग्रे । ३. क. °नाभिते । ४. अ. पादमध्यम । ५. अ.क.ग. जानुश्च्व । ६. अ.ग. पिप्फली । ७. क.ग.मुह्णुर्ण्णि° । ८. अ. °मध्येन । क.ग. °गुल्पोरु° । ९. ग. देसे देसे । १०. अ.क. प्रमानन्तु । ग. प्रनन्तु । ११. अ.ग. चीवराधार° । क. चीवराधर° । १२. अ. °त्सनभ्यान्तं । क. °बाह्यस्थनाक्षा च । ग. मुखनाश्यस्थणक्षा च । ज. मुखबाह्ये° । १३. अ. नीत्वा च यवाष्टकम् । ज. नीत्वावयवम् अष्टकम् । क.ग. नीत्वा यवम° । १४. अ.क.ग. चोरुमध्यतत् । १५. अ.क.ग. एवं जानु° । १६. ज. कर्णपार्श्वे च । १७. अ.क.ग. नीत्वन्तु । १८. अ.क.ग. त्रयङ्गु° । १९. अ.क.ग. ऊरुबाह्येस्तथैव च । २०. अ.क.ग. एतत् । २१. अ. कर्कटाभयाङ्गुष्टमन्तं । क.ग. °ययाङ्गुष्टमन्तरियं । २२. विंशद्वङ्गुल° ।

[The Plumbline Measurements]

69. One shall suspend the *madhya-sūtra* along the middle of the head, in front of the nose, along the chest, the navel and the generative organ and between the knees and the feet.

70. One shall suspend the *pārśva-sūtra* between the pippalī[1] and outer edge of the head, along the side of the arm region and along the middle of the thigh, the knee and the ankle.

71. Three times the breadth of any particular part [of the body shall be] equal to the measurement of the girth [of that part][2]. The hand holding the robe [shall reach] as high as the same arm.

72. The *abhaya-hasta*[3] [shall be] in line with the limits of the chin, the cheek and the tip of the nose. The projection[4] from the edge of the face and the nipple of the breast [shall be] eight *yavas*.

73. One shall suspend the *kaṭi-sūtra* by the side of the little finger [of the *kaṭaka-hasta*], along the middle of the hip and of the thigh and, likewise along the edge of the knee.

74. The projection from the outer edge of the ear [shall be] six *aṅgulas*, from the edge of the armpit three *aṅgulas* and from the upper arm also the same (i.e., three *aṅgulas*).

75. The *abhaya-hasta* is depicted in accordance with these *sūtra* measurements. The interval between [the thumb of] the *kaṭaka-hasta*[5] and the thumb of the *abhaya-hasta* is said to be twenty-two *aṅgulas*.

---

1. The short cartilaginous process attached to the inner end of the cheek, situated at the entrance to the hole of the ear; the antitragus.
2. Cf. *The Citrakarmaśāstra*, xiv.38.
3. The hand-gesture signifying granting of fearlessness or safety, in which the hand is held close to the body with the fully stretched palm with the fingers held together turned outwards.
4. That is, distance from the different limbs to the *sūtra*.
5. The hand-gesture in which the middle and the ring fingers are bent forward and the remaining three fingers but slightly bent. It signifies the holding of the robe.

स्तनाक्षात्तलपार्श्वे[1] च द्व्यन्तरमष्टमात्रकम्[2] ।
बाहुन्वाङ्गुष्ठमन्तर्यं[3] कोलकत्रयमुच्यते ।।७६।।

प्रकोष्ठमूलसन्धेश्चो[4]दरमध्येषु[5] द्व्यन्तरम् ।
बाणाङ्गुलं विशेषेण[6] वेदाङ्गुलमुच्यते ।।७७।।

कक्षाभयाङ्गुष्ठमन्तर्यं[7] चाष्टमात्रं विधीयते ।
स्तनाक्षात्तलपार्श्वे च द्व्यन्तरञ्च[8] तथैव च ।।७८।।

मुखान्ते[9] पिप्पलीदेशे[10] कण्ठपार्श्वे स्तने तथा[11] ।
श्रोणिकटिप्रदेशान्ते[12] तलमध्ये प्रलम्बयेत् ।।७९।।

कर्णबाह्ये[13] स्तनबाह्ये[14] चोरुजङ्घाप्रदेशके[15] ।
नलकाबाह्यदेशे चानामिकान्ते[16] प्रलम्बयेत् ।।८०।।

कक्षसन्धिकटिपार्श्वे जङ्घान्ते च तथैव च ।
कनिष्ठाङ्गुलिपार्श्वे[17] च लम्बयेत् कक्षसूत्रकम् ।।८१।।

बाहुमध्ये तदग्रान्ते तलबाह्ये[18] प्रलम्बयेत् ।
(तद्)बाहुपार्श्वे[19] प्रकोष्ठान्ते[20] बाहुसूत्रम्प्रलम्बयेत् ।।८२।।

---

१. ग. स्तनाक्षतल° । ज. °पार्श्वञ्च । २. अ. द्वान्तरञ्चाष्ट° । ग. द्वन्तरामाष्ट° । ज. द्व्यन्तरञ्चाष्ट° । ३. अ.क.ग. बाहुद्वाङ्गुष्ट° । ४. अ.क.ग. °ष्टमूलसन्धिश्च । ५. अ.ग. °मध्येसु । ज. °मध्ये । ६. क. °ङ्गुल विशेषाणि । ज. ङ्गुलविशेषेण । ७. अ. कक्षादभयाङ्गुष्टमन्त° । क. °ष्टमन्तर्य । ग. °ङ्गुष्ट अन्तर्यं च । ज. कक्षाद् अङ्गुष्ठ अन्तर्य्यं । ८. अ. द्वान्तरञ्च । ग. द्वन्तरा च । ज. द्व्यन्तरन्तु । ९. अ.क. मुखान्तरम् । ग. मुखान्तं । १०. अ.क. पिप्फली° । ११. अ.क. स्तनान्तथा । १२. अ. श्रोनिकटिप्रदेशान्तात् । १३. अ. कर्णबाणह्ये । १४. अ. स्तनाबाह्ये । ज. स्तने बाह्ये । १५. अ. चोरुजङ्गा° । १६. अ. नामिकन्ते । क. नामिकान्ते । १७. क. कनिष्टा° । अ. कणिष्टा° । १८. क. णलबाह्ये । १९. अ.क.ग. प्रकोष्टान्ते । २०. अ.क. तद्वाहु° ।

76. The distance between the nipple of the breast and the side of the palm [of the *abhaya* hand shall] also [be] eight *aṅgulas*. The interval between the arm and the thumb is said to be three *kolakas*.

77. The interval between the point where the root of the hand touches the arm and the mid-belly is said to be specifically five *aṅgulas* or four *aṅgulas*.

78. It is enjoined that the interval between the armpit and the thumb of the *abhaya-hasta* be eight *aṅgulas*. The interval between the nipple and the side of the palm shall also be the same.

79. One shall suspend [the *pārśva-sūtra*] along the extremity of the face, the *pippalī* region, by the side of the neck, through the breast, along the hip and the lions and the middle of the foot.

80. One shall suspend the *karṇasūtra* along the outer edge of the ear and of the breast, along the thigh and the shank, the outer edge of the ankle and by the side of the fourth toe.

81. One shall suspend the *kakṣa-sūtra* through the armpit, by the side of the hip, along the extremity of the shank and by the side of the little toe.

82. One shall suspend [the *kaṣabhāhya-sūtra*] along the middle of the arm and the edge of the fore-arm and outside the palm; and one shall suspend the *bāhu-sūtra* by the side of the same arm and outside the fore-arm.

शिरोमध्ये[1] ककुन्मध्ये[2] पृष्ठमध्ये[3] पार्ष्ण्यन्तरे[4] ।
परभागे[5] मध्यसूत्रं[6] योजयेत् तद्विचक्षणः[7] ।।८३।।

कर्णपार्श्वे [च] स्फिग्मध्ये[8] नलकान्तरयोर्विदुः[9] ।
कक्षसन्धि[10]कटिपार्श्वे[11] जानुपार्श्वे[12] प्रलम्बयेत् ।।८४।।

लम्बस्य हीनेषु[13] च कर्तृरोगान्[14]
उपमानहीनेषु[15] धनायुनाशनम्[16] ।
शुद्धौ[17] तु कृत्वा नृपपक्षवृद्धिम्
कर्तुश्च[18] सर्वम् परिपालयन्तु ।।८५।।

[निषण्णबिम्बविधिः ।]
अथ ऊर्ध्वम्[19] प्रवक्ष्यामि[20] योगासनं[21] विशेषतः[22] ।
नासाग्रे[23] दत्तदृष्टिं च[24] पार्ष्ण्यङ्गुष्ठावलोकनम्[25] ।।८६।।

निषण्णम्[26] भवाङ्गचित्तन्[27] तूपनैःस्पृह्यं[28] निरोधकम्[29] ।
यावत् पादादिकेशान्तन्[30] तावन्निर्गममिष्यते[31] ।।८७।।

---

१. क.ग. सिरोमध्ये । २. अ.क. ककुधमध्ये । ग. ककुद° । ३. अ.क.ग. पृष्ट° । ४. अ. क.ग. पाष्णिरन्तरे । ५. ग. प्रभागे । ६. अ.क.ग. मध्यसूत्रानि । ७. ज. तद्विचक्षणैः । ८. अ. स्तनमध्ये । क. स्थनमध्ये । ग. संनिथमध्ये । ज. स्फिकामध्ये । ९. क. °न्तरयो विदुः । अ.ग. °न्तरयो विधुः । १०. अ. कक्षसन्धौ । क. कक्षसन्धे । ग. कक्षसन्धै । ११. ज. °कटीपार्श्वे । १२. अ. °पार्श्वे च । १३. अ. हीनेसु । क.ग. हीणेषु । १४. अ. कर्तृञ्च रोगान् । क. कर्त्तुरो° । ग. कत्रु रो° । १५. अ. मानहीनेसु । क. मुपमान° । १६. क. ग. °नासनम् । १७. ग. सुधौ । १८. अ. कर्तृञ्च । क.ग. क्रत्वा च । १९. क.ग. ऊर्ध्वं । २०. क.ग. प्रवक्षामि । २१. क. योगाशण । ग. °सन । २२. क. विशेषन । ग. विसेसतत् । २३. क. नासागेद् । २४. क. दगदिष्टेव । ग. दानदृष्टे च । २५. क. पार्ष्णाङ्गुष्टवलोचनम् । ग. पासनंगुष्टावलोचनम् । २६. क. निषणम् । ग. निसन्यम् । २७. ग. भाङ्गचित्तन्तु । २८. क. उपनिष्मुतम् । ग. उपणिष्मुतम् । २९. ग. णिरो° । ३०. क.ग. °केसान्तम् । ३१. ग. °मिश्यते ।

83. The wise one shall employ the *madhya-sūtra* at the back along the middle of the *uṣṇīṣa* and the head, the middle of the back and between the two heels.

84. They knew the *pārśva-sūtra* [to fall] by the side of the ear, along the middle of the buttocks and through the middle of the ankle. One shall suspend the *kakṣa-sūtra* through the armpit, along the side of the hip and outside the knee region.

85. When the plumbline measurements fall short the builder will be afflicted with disease, and when the interior measurements (*upamāna*) fall short there will be loss of wealth and the life span will be reduced. [Therefore] having rendered [the six kinds of measurement] clean, [the artisan] shall ensure welfare of the ruler and protect everything pertaining to the builder. [The Sedent Image]

86. I shall next deal with the *yogāsana*[1] in particular, with the gaze fixed at the tip of the nose and [seeming to be] looking at the heel and the thumb.

87. It is desired that the seated image betraying mind fixed on *bhavāṅga*, free from passion and completely pacified, has a projection[2] equal to the distance between the hair-limit and the feet.

---

1. Image depicting seated figure in meditative posture.
2. This refers to the distance between the two outstretched knees of the seated figures.

आसनात्[१] केशपर्यन्तं[२] षष्टिद्व्यर्धाङ्गुलम्भवेत्[३] ।
सर्वावयवसंयुक्तं कुर्यात् तत्रैव[४] बुद्धिमान्[५] ।।८८।।

अधो वामपादं[६] स्याद्[७] अवामोपरिशायिते[८] ।
एवं हस्तसमं[९] कुर्याद् भावसौम्याङ्गशोभनम्[१०] ।।८९।।

हस्तपादोदयं वक्त्रं तत्तुल्यं निर्गमम्भवेत्[११] ।
तदूर्ध्वन्नाभिमेढ्राच्च[१२] भागमेवं प्रयोजयेत् ।।९०।।

हिक्कानाभिहृदयान्तं सप्तविंशाङ्गुलम्भवेत् ।
हिक्काद् ग्रीवान्तरं हीनम्[१३] भागम् पर्वणा एव[१४] च ।।९१।।

गलमर्धाङ्गुलम्प्रोक्तं वक्त्रं त्रयोदशार्धकम् ।
त्र्यङ्गुलन्तु[१५] शिरोत्तुङ्गम् मूर्धनि अध्यर्धाङ्गुलम्[१६] ।।९२।।

त्रिविधं[१७] निषण्णमेवं[१८] स्यात्[१९] कुर्यात् तत्रैव[२०] बुद्धिमान्।
जानुद्व्यन्तरसूत्रन्तु[२१] निम्नम्[२२] पर्वचतुर्थकम् ।।९३।।

ऊर्ध्वपादं[२३] त्रिमात्रं स्यान् निर्गमाधरमेव[२४] च ।
द्व्यर्धम्[२५] अङ्गुष्ठदीर्घन्तु[२६] तलतारं[२७] षडङ्गुलम्[२८] ।।९४।।

---

१. अ. आशनात् । क. आसनन् । २. क. तेतपर्य° । ग. केस° । ३. अ. षष्ट्यर्धाङ्गुल° । क. शष्टिर्द्विङ्गुल° । ग. °द्विर्धाङ्गुल° । ४. क. तत्रेव । ग. प्रात्रैव । ५. अ. बुद्धिमां । ६. क. वामपाद । ७. अ.क.ग. श्यात् । ज. शय्याम् । ८. अ.क.ग. °सायिते । ९. ग. हस्तयवं । १०. अ. सौम्याङ्घसोभनम् । ग. °सवुम्याङ्गसोभनम् । ११. ग. णन्तुल्यं णिर्ग° । १२. अ. तदूर्धन्नाभि° । क. तदर्धन्नाहमेढ्रा च । ग. तदूर्धं नाभिमेढ्रा च । १३. ग. हीणम् । १४. अ. ग. पर्वमिव । क. पार्श्वमिव । ज. भागम् पर्वणा हीनमेव । १५. अ. त्रयाङ्गुलन्तु । क.ग. त्रयङ्गुलन्तु । १६. अ. अध्यर्धाङ्गुलम्मूर्धनि । क.ग. द्यर्धाङ्गुलमूर्धसु । ज. अद्ध यर्धाङ्गुलमूर्धनि । १७. ज. त्रिधा । १८. अ. निसन्नवेवं । १९. ब. श्यात् । २०. ग. तथेहि । २१. अ.ग. जानुद्वयसूत्रन्तु । क. जानुद्वसूत्रन्तु । २२. ग. निमणं । २३. अ. ऊर्धपादं । क. ऊर्धपादन् । ग. ऊर्धपाद । ज. ऊर्ध्वपादस् । २४. अ. निर्गधमारमेव । ज. निर्गमाधर एव । २५. क. द्यर्धम् । ग. ध्यर्धम् । २६. क. अङ्गुष्ट° । ग. आङ्गुष्टदीब्रन्तु । ज. अङ्गुष्ठनीव्रन्तु । २७. अ. तलातारं । क. नलकारा । ग. नलतार । २८. ग. सडाङ्गुलम् । अ. षडाङ्गुलं तलातारं । दीर्घमङ्गुष्ठमर्धकम् ।

88. [The distance] from the seat to the hair-limit shall be sixty-two and a half *aṅgulas*. The wise one shall endow the same with all [essential] features.
89. The left leg shall lie underneath [while] the right [leg] rests above [it]. One shall, likewise symmetrically position the two hands [with the image] looking serene on account of its gentle nature.
90. The height of the hands and the feet [shall be] one face-length and the projection shall be equal to it. One shall allow one *bhāga* above that from the *meḍhra* up to the navel.
91. [The distance] from the hiccup to the navel through the chest shall be twenty-seven *aṅgulas*. From the hiccup up to the [upper] limit of the neck [there shall be] one *bhāga* short of one *aṅgula* [i.e., 3½ *aṅgulas*].
92. The *gala* is declared [to measure] half an *aṅgula* and the face thirteen and a half *aṅgulas*. The height of the head [shall be] three *aṅgulas* and the excrescence [on the head] one and a half *aṅgulas*.
93. So shall be the seated image which is of three types. The wise one shall make [them] in the said manner. The recession of the *sūtra* drawn across the two knees [shall be] four *aṅgulas*.
94. The upper foot shall be three *aṅgulas* [in height] and the projection of the lower [foot] shall also be the same. The width of the foot [shall be] six *aṅgulas* and the length of the big toe two and a half *aṅgulas*.

मेढ्रपार्ष्ण्यन्तरन्नेत्रम्[1] पादपार्ष्णिषु[2] निर्गमम् ।
[द्व्यर्धमङ्गुष्ठनीव्रन्तु त्र्यङ्गुलम्पादनिर्गमम्] ।।९५।।
वामपादस्तथैकं स्यात् क्रमान् निर्गममाद्रियेत् ।।९५½।।

जानुद्व्यन्तरगुल्फादिशिरान्तं[3] तुङ्गमेव च ।
जानुद्वोपरिबाहुश्च[4] तुल्यम्प्रमाणमुच्यते[5] ।।९६।।

बाहुस्तनान्तरञ्चैव अङ्गुलद्वयमुच्यते ।
उदरमध्ये च बाहुश्च[6] प्रकोष्ठमूलसन्धिका[7] ।।९७।।
तस्य द्व्यन्तरमानन्तु[8] पञ्चमात्रम्प्रकीर्तितम् ।।९७½।।

कूर्परात्[9] कटिपार्श्वन्तु[10] चतुर्मात्रम्प्रशस्यते[11] ।
मणिसन्धेर्[12] वस्त्यन्तर्यन्[13] नेत्रमेकाङ्गुलम्भवेत्[14] ।।९८।।

कक्षात्[15] प्रकोष्ठ-म्-अग्रन्तु[16] नयनाधिकवक्त्रकम्[17] ।
कूर्परान्[18] मणिसन्धिश्च[19] द्विमात्राधिकवक्त्रकम् ।।९९।।

शीर्षस्य[20] चतुष्पार्श्वेन[21] वक्त्रमेकं घनम्भवेत् ।
ग्रीवमेवं[22] नव[23] कुर्याद् हृदयन्[24] त्रयोदशार्धकम्[25] ।।१००।।

---

१. अ. मेढ्रत् पार्ष्ण्यन्तर° । क.ग. मेढ्रपार्ष्ण्यन्तर । २. अ.क.ग. पादपार्ष्णेषु । ३. अ. जानुद्वान्तर° । क.ग. जानुद्वन्तरगुल्पादिसिरान्तम् । ४. अ. जानुवोपरि° । क. जानुद्वौपरि° । क.ग. °बाहुस्च । ज. °द्वोपरि बाहू च । ५. क. तुल्यतुम्मार्णि° । ग. तुल्यन्तुम्मार्णि° । ज. तुल्यन्वतुम्मार्णिम् उच्यते । ६. अ. मध्योदरबाहुश्च । क. उदरमध्ये बाहुश्च । ग. °बाहुस्च । ७. अ.क.ग. प्रकोष्टमूलन्तु सन्धिका । ८. अ. तस्य द्वान्तर° । क. तस्या द्वन्त° । ग. तस्य द्वन्त° । ९. अ.ग. कूर्परा । १०. अ.क. °पार्श्वेन । ११. ग. चतुम्मार्णिम्प्र° । १२. अ. मणिसन्ध्याद् । क.ग. मनिसन्ध्याद् । १३. अ. वस्त्यन्त । क. वस्तिरन्तर्य । ग. द्वयन्तर्यन् । ज. वणिसन्ध्यावस्तिमन्तर्य्यं । १४. क. णेत्रमेका° । १५. अ. कक्षत् । ग. कक्षां । १६. अ. प्रकोष्टाग्रमानं । क.ग. प्रकोष्टाग्रन्तु । ज. प्रकोष्ठमग्रेण । १७. अ. वक्त्रं नयनाधिकम्मतं । ग. णयना° । १८. अ. कूर्परात् । क. कूर्प्परा । ग. कूर्प्पार । १९. अ. °सन्धिकस्च । क.ग. मनि° । ज. °सन्धिञ्च । २०. क. शीर्षश्य । ग. शीर्षे । २१. अ. चतुपार्श्वेण । क. चतुपार्श्वानि । ग. चतुपार्श्वे । २२. क. ग्रीवमेवा । २३. अ. नवङ् । क. नवं । २४. क. हृदये । ग. हृदयान् । २५. अ. त्रिदशा° ।

95. The distance from the *meḍhra* to the heel [shall be] two *aṅgulas*, and the projection of the heel [too shall be the same]. The length of the thumb [shall be] two and a half *aṅgulas* and the projection of the foot three *aṅgulas*. The left foot shall similarly be one *aṅgula*, and one shall recommend the projection in the proper manner.

96. The distance between the two knees shall be equal to the height from the ankle to the hair-limit. The distance from the two knees to the roots of the arm are said to be equal. The interval between the arm and the breast is said to be two *aṅgulas*.

97. The distance from the mid-belly to the arm as well as to the joint of the arm and the fore-arm is declared to be five *aṅgulas*.

98. It is commendable that [the distance] from the elbow to the hip be four *aṅgulas*. The interval between the wrist and the lower belly shall be three *aṅgulas*.

99. The distance from the armpit to the end of the fore-arm shall be one face-length and two *aṅgulas*. [The distance] from the elbow to the wrist [shall also be] two *aṅgulas* more than a face-length.

100. The thickness of the head from all the four sides shall be one face-length. Similarly, one shall make the neck nine [*aṅgulas*] and the chest thirteen and a half [*aṅgulas*].

उदरञ्चाष्टद्वयं[१] कुर्याद् वस्तिर्[२] नवद्वयम्भवेत्[३] ।
तलपृष्ठस्य[४] विस्तारम् पञ्चदशकला[५] भवेत् ।।१०१।।

कक्षात्[६] स्तनोन्नतञ्चैव[७] कोलकद्वयमेव च ।
मध्योदरस्य[८] नीव्रन्तु[९] दशैकाङ्गुलमेव च ।।१०२।।
प्रकोष्ठान्[१०] मेढ्रनीव्रन्तु[११] द्वादशाङ्गुलमुच्यते ।।१०२½।।

मूर्ध्निमध्ये च[१२] नासाग्रे[१३] हृदये मेढ्रनाभिके[१४] ।
अङ्गुष्ठपर्वमध्ये[१५] च पादयोरक्षमध्यमे[१६] ।।१०३।।

मध्यसूत्रमिति[१७] ज्ञेयं[१८] तस्य[१९] द्व्यन्तरमुच्यते[२०] ।
उष्णीषाद्[२१] द्वादशाङ्गुल्यम् पुरस्ताद् अवलम्बितम् ।।१०४।।

सूत्राल्ललाटमध्ये तु[२२] अन्तरम् मात्रकत्रयम्[२३] ।
नासाग्रेणाङ्गुलं[२४] गोजिमूले[२५] त्र्यङ्गुलम्भवेत्[२६] ।।१०५।।

हनुचक्रं[२७] तथैवं स्याद्[२८] ग्रीवाग्रेषु च[२९] सप्तकम् ।
त्रियवाधिकसप्तन्तु हिक्कामूलेषु[३०] अन्तरम्[३१] ।।१०६।।

---

१. अ. अष्टद्वयोदशङ् । २. अ. वस्तीम् । क. वस्तिन् । ग. वस्तिं । ३. अ. अष्टादशम्भवेत् । ४. अ. °पृष्टस्य । क.ग. तलाप्रिष्टस्य । ५. अ.क.ग. पञ्चादश° । ६. क. कक्षस्या । ग. कक्ष° । ७. अ. °न्नतिञ्चैव । क. °न्नतकञ्चैव । ८. क. °दरस्या । ग. मध्येदरश्या । ९. अ. दीर्घन्तु । क. दिव्रन्तु । ग. दिव्रर्त्तन्तु । १०. अ. प्रकोष्टाण् । क.ग. प्रकोष्ट° । ११. अ. मेढ्रदीर्घन्तु । क. °दीव्रन्तु । ग. दिव्रर्त्तन्तु । १२. क. मुहुर्ण्णि मध्ये । ग. मुहुन्निमद्धे च । १३. अ. नास्याग्रे । १४. क.ग. मेड्र° । १५. अ.क.ग. अङ्गुष्टौ पर्व° । ज. अङ्गुष्ठौ पर्व्व° । १६. अ. द्वौपादक्षममध्यमे । ज. द्विपादावक्ष° । १७. ग. मध्यसूत्रन्ति । १८. क. ज्ञेय्यं १९. क. तस्स । ग. तश्य । २०. अ. द्वान्तर° । क.ग. द्वन्तर° । २१. अ. उष्णीसा । क.ग. मुष्णीष । २२. अ.क. °मध्येषु । ग. °मद्धेषु । २३. क. मात्रतत्रयं । ग. मात्रान्त्रयं । २४. अ. नासात्रमङ्गुल्यङ् । क. °ग्रेण अङ्गुल्यम् । ग. °ग्रेन अङ्गुलम् । ज. नासिकाग्रेण चाङ्गुल्यम् । २५. अ. °मूल । क. °मूल । ग. °मूलत् । २६. त्रयाङ्गुल्यम्भ° । क. त्रयंगुलम् । ग. त्रयंगुलं । २७. क. हनुचक्रेषु । ग. हनुचक्रेसु । २८. अ. तथैव श्याद् । क.ग. श्यात् । २९. क.ग. ग्रीवाग्रेसु । ज. ग्रीवाग्रेण च । ३०. क. °मूलसु । ग. °मूलेसु । ३१. ग. अन्तरं । ज. चान्तरम् ।

101. One shall make the mid-belly sixteen *aṅgulas* wide and the lower belly shall be eighteen *aṅgulas*. The width of the *talapṛṣṭha*[1] shall be fifteen *kalās* [i.e., thirty *aṅgulas*].

102. The elevation of the breast from the armpit shall be two *kolakas*. The height of the mid-belly [shall be] eleven *aṅgulas*. The height of the root of the *meḍhra* from the fore-arm is said to be twelve *aṅgulas*.

103 The plumbline suspended along the middle of the *uṣṇīṣa*,
104. the tip of the nose, the chest, the navel and the *meḍhra*, in between the links of the two thumbs and through the middle of the ankles [of the two feet] should be known to be the *madhya-sūtra*. The interspace measurements with regard to it shall [now] be stated. It is suspended twelve *aṅgulas* away from the *uṣṇīṣa*.

105. The distance from the *sūtra* to the middle of the forehead [shall be] three *aṅgulas*. It (i.e., the *sūtra*) shall be one *aṅgula* from the tip of the nose and three *aṅgulas* from the base of the *gojī*.

106. The *hanucakra* shall be similar (i.e., three *aṅgulas* away from the *sūtra* and [the interspace measurement] at the upper end of the neck seven [*aṅgulas*]. The interval between [the *sūtra* and] the base of the hiccup [shall be] seven *aṅgulas* and three *yavas*.

---

1. The width of the seat, that is, the distance from the knee to the back along the sides.

हृदयात्[1] तत्सूत्रमन्तर्यम्[2] अङ्गुलत्रयमेव च ।
मध्योदरेण[3] चाङ्गुल्यं[4] स्पर्शयेन्[5] मेढ्रमेव च[6] ।।१०७।।

एतत्सूत्रं[7] यथा कुर्याद् योगासनमिति[8] स्मृतम् ।
वक्त्रबाह्ये[9] स्तनाक्षाच्च[10] मणिसन्धिषु[11] बाह्यतः ।।१०८।।
जङ्घाग्रतस्तु लम्बित्वा पार्श्वसूत्रं विधीयते[12] ।।१०८½।।

कक्षसन्धिकटिपार्श्वे जङ्घान्ते च तथैव च ।
कूर्परागे च लम्बित्वा कक्षसूत्रं विधीयते ।।१०९।।
एतत्सूत्रमिदं ज्ञात्वा[13] लम्बयेद्विधिना गुरुः[14] ।।१०९½।।

मूर्ध्निमध्ये[15] च कर्णान्ते[16] बाहुपार्श्वे च कूर्परे ।
एतत्पार्श्वसूत्रन्तु[17] निषण्णत्रयमेव[18] च ।।११०।।

बिम्बायामत्रिभागैकं[19] चतुर्भागैकभागिकम्[20] ।
पञ्चभागैकभागं वा[21] आसनं[22] तुङ्गमुच्यते ।।१११।।

---

१. अ. हृदयन्तात् । क.ग. हृदयान्तत् । २. ग. °मन्तर्य । ३. अ. मध्योदर । ४. अ. नवाङ्गुल्यम् । ५. अ. सप्तन्तु । क. स्तपव । ग. स्पष । ६. क. मेड्रमेव च । ७. अ. ग.ज. एतत्सूत्र° । क. एतं सूत्रं । ८. क.ग. °सणमिति । ९. अ. °बाह्य । क. वक्त्रबाह्यश्च । ग. वक्त्रं बाह्य । १०. अ. स्तनाक्षा च । क. स्तनक्षा च । ग. चनाक्षा च । ११. क. मनिसन्धिसु । ग. मनिसन्धि । १२. क. कक्षसूत्रं वि° । ग. कक्षसूत्र वि° । ज. मुखान्तं प्रवि° । १३. क. °दत्वा । ग. °विदं दत्वा । १४. क. °गुरु । १५. मुर्धनी° । क. मुहुर्णि° । ग. मुर्त्तिमध्ये । १६. क.ग. कर्ण्णन्ते । १७. ज. एतेन पार्श्व° । १८. अ. निसन्नयस्त्रय° । क. निषन्यत्रयं° । ग. निसन्त्रय° । १९. अ. बिम्बायामं त्रिभागैक । ज. बिम्बायामात् त्रिभा° । २०. ग. °भणकम् । २१. अ. भागं च । क. भागं । ग. भागं स्यात् । २२. अ. आसनां । ग. आसणं ।

107. The *sūtra* shall be three *aṅgulas* from the chest, one *aṅgula* from the mid-belly and touches the *meḍhra*.

108. [When] one shall suspend this *sūtra* in that manner it is known as the *yogāsana* [position]. [The plumbline] suspended along the outer edge of the face, the nipple of the breast, the outer edge of the wrist and in front of the shank is enjoined to be the *pārśvasūtra*.

109. [The plumbline] suspended through the armpit, along the side of the hip, at the end of the shank, and similarly in front of the elbow is known as the *kakṣa-sūtra*. Having known this *sūtra* in this manner, the teacher shall suspend it in the proper manner.

110. This *pārśvasūtra* may be suspended in three ways, i.e., along the middle of the *uṣṇīṣa*, at the inner edge of the ear and the side of the arm and the elbow.

111. The height of the seat is said to be one-third, one-fourth or one-fifth of the height (lit., length) of the image.

[शयनासनलक्षणम् ।]

अथ ऊर्ध्वम्[१] प्रवक्ष्यामि[२] शयनानान्तु[३] लक्षणम् ।
श्रेष्ठेषु[४] योगशय्यां[५] [च] बिम्बानां[६] योग्यतः[७] कुरु[८] ।।११२।।

बिम्बे मर्मप्रदेशन्तु[९] हित्वारोपणसन्धिकम्[१०] ।
उक्तमार्गेण[११] कर्तव्यं सर्वसम्पत्तिवर्धनम् ।।११३।।
विरुद्धमेव कृतञ्चैव[१२] स्थानभ्रंशायुनाशनम्[१३] ।।११३½।।

यावद्[१४] हर्म्यस्य[१५] चायामं[१६] षोडशांशं[१७] विशेषतः[१८] ।
तावद् भागद्वयञ्चैव[१९] द्विपार्श्वे[२०] द्व्यन्तरम्भवेत्[२१] ।।११४।।

गृहाणां[२२] सप्त विस्तारं शयनं स्यात्[२३] त्र्यर्धकम्[२४] ।
ब्रह्मात्[२५] पिशाचपादार्धे[२६] शयनतारम्[२७] प्रशस्यते ।।११५।।

वदनं[२८] पञ्चमं[२९] कुर्यात् त्रिभागं शयनोदयम्[३०] ।
शयनात्[३१] पार्श्वदेशन्तु[३२] वंशसूत्रान्तरम्भवेत्[३३] ।।११६।।

कोलकं तन्नीत्वा तु[३४] सर्वसम्पत्तिवर्धनम् ।
सूत्रयोर्[३५] निर्गति शयनं[३६] सर्वभोगायुनाशनम्[३७] ।।११७।।

---

१. ग. ऊर्धम् । २. क. पवक्षामि । ३. अ. शयनासन । क. शयनानन्तु । ग. सयनानन्तु। ४. अ. श्रेष्टषु। क.ग. श्रेष्टेसु । ज. श्रेष्ठे तु । ५. ज. योगशय्याश्च । ६. क. बिम्बाणं। ग. बिम्बानं। ७. क.ग. योग्यते । ज. योग्यत्वे। ८. क.ग. गुरुः । अ. कुर्याद्बिम्बञ्च योग्यताम्। ९. अ.क. बिम्बप्रमाणदेशन्तु । ग. येमप्रदेसन्तु । १०. क.ग. नीत्वा° । ज. नीत्वा°। °सन्धिकात् । ११. अ.क. °मार्गेन । १२. ज. कृत्वा च । १३. अ. °भ्रंश्यायुनासनम् । ग. °भ्रुश्यायुनासनम् । १४. अ. तावत् । १५. अ. हम्याश्य । ग. हम्यास्या । १६. ग. वयामं। १७. अ. सोडन्‌श । क. षोडशंश । ग. शोडशांश । १८. अ. विषेसतः । १९. अ. °द्वयं न्चैव। २०. अ. °पार्श्वे च । २१. अ. द्वान्तरम् । क. द्वन्तरम् । ग. द्वन्तर । २२. अ. ग्रहनाम्। क. ग्रहानं । ग. ग्रह्मनां । २३. क. सयना श्यात् । ग. सयनाश्य । ज. शयनस्य । २४. अ.क.ग. त्रयार्धकम् । २५. क.ग. ब्रह्मा । २६. क. पिशाचा पदर्धे च। ग. पिसाच पदार्धे च । २७. क. शयनातारम् । ग. सयनतारं । २८. ग. वदणं । २९. ज. वदनपञ्चमात्। ३०. अ.ग. सयनो° । ३१. अ.ग. सयनात् । ३२. अ. पार्श्वे देशन्तु । ग. पर्वदि° । ३३. क. वससूत्रा° । ३४. अ.ग. तन्नीत्वन्तु । क. तर्त्तित्वन्तु । ३५. अ. सूत्रयो। क. पुत्रयो। ग. सूत्रयोनि । ३६. अ. °ते सयनम् । क. निर्ग्ग सयनम् । ग. निग्गति । ज. निर्ग्गतिकत्वात् । ३७. अ.क.ग. °नासनम् ।

[The Recumbent Image]

112. I shall next set out the [special] features of the recumbent image. One shall execute recumbent images of noble personages in reclining position [and absorbed] in deep meditation.

113. Avoiding the vital points in the image should the *stambhāropaṇa-sandhika* be executed. If done in the prescribed manner, there will be increase of all prosperity. [If] done in a manner contrary [to this], the destruction of the place and the diminishing of the life span [of the builder will follow].

114. When the length of the [image-] house [consists of] sixteen parts, two parts on both sides shall be interspaces (empty).

115. Seven [parts shall be] the width of the house; the *śayana* shall occupy three and a half [of them]. The width of the *śayana* extending from the *brahma-pāda* up to half of *paiśāca-pāda* is commendable.

116. [If] the face-length [consists of] five [parts] one shall make the *śayana* three parts high. The side region shall lie between the *śayana* and the *vaṃśa-sūtra*.

117. [If] two *aṅgulas* are left out from that *sūtra* there will be increase of all prosperity. When the *śayana* projects away from the two *sūtras*, the destruction of all crops and life [will follow].

अधःकर्णस्य[१] पिप्पल्यां[२] नालपार्श्वे च नाभिके ।
मध्ये[३] योनेश्च[४] जान्वोश्च[५] मध्यमम्पादयुग्मके ।।११८।।

मूर्ध्निमध्ये[६] ललाटे च नासामध्ये[७] स्तनान्तके[८] ।
पार्श्वकटिकमाश्रित्य[९] मुखसूत्रम्प्रहारयेत् ।।११९।।

मूर्ध्नि स्कन्धबाह्ये[१०] च कूर्परे[११] मणिसन्धिषु[१२] ।
मध्यमाङ्गुलिगुल्फे च[१३] विज्ञेयम् पार्श्वसूत्रकम् ।।१२०।।

बाहुमूलतलान्ते च उदरपार्श्वे[१४] च[१५] सूत्रकम्[१६] ।
जानुकाच्च[१७] षडङ्गुल्यं[१८] कटेश्च[१९] चतुरङ्गुलम्[२०] ।।१२१।।
स्तनान्ताच्चतुरङ्गुल्यं[२१] वंशसूत्रम्प्रयोजयेत् ।।१२१½।।

पादान्तरन्तु[२२] नेत्रं स्याच् चर्म[२३] सर्वाभिसम्मतम् ।
चर्मात्[२४] स्तनोच्चमानन्तु[२५] कोलकत्रयमुच्यते ।।१२२।।

स्तनान्तरस्य[२६] मानन्तु[२७] मात्रमेकादशम्भवेत्[२८] ।
कुटिबाहोर्[२९] नवाङ्गुल्यन्[३०] तारमेवं[३१] विधीयते ।।१२३।।

---

१. अ.क.ग. अधोकर्ण्ण। २. अ. पिप्फ च । क.ग. पिप्फली च। ३. क. मर्ध्ये । ग. मध्य°। ४. अ.क.ग. योनि। ५. अ. जानेम च । क. जन्वा च । ग. जन्मा च । ६. क. मुहुर्ण्णि°। ग. मुहुर्न्नि° । ७. अ. नासिमध्ये । क. नासमध्ये । ग. नाभिमध्ये । ८. ग. स्तान्तके । ९. अ. कटिकपार्श्वमाश्रित्य । क. पार्श्वकटिराश्रित्य । ग. पार्श्वकटिकराश्रित्य । ज. पार्श्वकटीराश्रित्य । १०. ग. सखन्धबाह्यो च । This verse is not found in अ. क has only the second line, but the latter half of the first line has been preserved in Com.

११. ग. कूपरि । १२. क. मणिसन्धि । ग. मनिसन्धिसु । १३. क.ग. मध्यमाङ्गुलि । १४. ग. उदरपार्श्व । १५. ज. तत् । १६. अ. पार्श्वे चोदरसूत्रकम् । १७. अ. जानुकन्व । क. ग. जानुका च । १८. अ.क. षडाङ्गुल° । ग. सडाङ्गु° । १९. ज. कटेश्च । २०. ग. चतुङ्गुलम्। २१. क. °तुरङ्गुलम् । २२. अ. पादास्तरण । क. पादंतर। ग. पादंन्तर। ज. पादान्तरेण। २३. ग. मर्म्म । २४. ग. मर्मात् । २५. अ. स्तनोच° । क.ग. स्तनौच्छमा° । २६. ग. °न्तरेश्य। २७. अ. मनन्तु । ग. माणन्तु । २८. क. °कादसम्भ° । २९. अ. क. कुटिलबाहु । ज. कुटिलबाहोर्। ३०. ग. नवाङ्गुल्लयं । ३१. ग. तारवेवन् ।

118. The *madhya-sūtra* [shall pass] along the *pippalī* of the lower ear, by the side of the lobe of the [same] ear, through the navel and the middle of the *meḍhra* and the between the two knees and the two feet.

119. One shall lay the *mukha-sūtra* through the middle of the *uṣṇīṣa*, of the forehead and of the nose, along the extremity of the breast and close to the side of the hip.

120. The *pārśva-sūtra* should be known [to be laid] along the side of the *uṣṇīṣa*, outside the neck, through the elbow and the wrist, along the ankle and through the middle toe.

121. The ḍistance from that *sūtra* (i.e., *vaṃśasūtra*) to the root of the arm, the end of the palm, the side of the belly and to the knee shall be six *aṅgulas* in each case. One shall lay the *vaṃśasūtra* at a distance of four *aṅgulas* from the hip and four *aṅgulas* from the breast-line.

122. The interval between the two feet shall be two *aṅgulas*. The *carma* has been recommended in all [*śilpa* texts]. The elevation of the nipple of the breast from the *carma* is said to be three *kolakas*.

123. The distance between the two [nipples of the] breasts shall be eleven *aṅgulas*. The width of the bent arm is prescribed to be nine *aṅgulas*.

कक्षात्[१] [तु] कूर्परान्तस्य[२] मानमेकादश[३] कला[:] ।
कूर्परान्[४] मणिसन्धिश्च[५] कोलका[६] नव-म्-एव[७] च ।।१२४।।

चूचुकात्[८] कूर्परान्तञ्च[९] कोलका [:] षट् प्रकीर्तिताः ।
अधोहस्ततलान्ते च नेत्रसूत्रम्प्रलम्बयेत् ।।१२५।।

अङ्गुष्ठात् कपोलाग्रञ्च[१०] स्कन्धनालावलम्बनम्[११] ।
अथोर्ध्वबाहुमूलन्तु[१२] अधःकक्षान्तरं[१३] समम्[१४] ।।१२६।।

बाहुमूलान्तरञ्चैव मणिसन्धि द्विमात्रकम्[१५] ।
उपरिकर्णनालञ्च[१६] कपोलाद् ग्रीवलम्बनम्[१७] ।।१२७।।

वक्त्राधारसमोत्तुङ्गं[१८] वदनोदयमेव च ।
वदनं [च] सम्पूर्णं[१९] स्यात्[२०] सर्वावयवशोभनम्[२१] ।।१२८।।

निषण्णे शयने स्थिते[२२] बिम्बं[२३] तादृशलक्षणम्[२४] ।
पूर्ववत्तारदीर्घन्तु[२५] कुर्यात् तथैव[२६] [बुद्धिमान्] ।।१२९।।

---

१. अ कक्षत् । २. अ. कुरापन्तस्य । क.ग. कूर्प्परान्तस्तु । ३. अ. °मेकादसा कला । क. मा [न] मेका° । ग. मार्णं एकादशाकला । ज. मानाद् एकादशां कलाम् । ४. क.ग. कूर्प्परा । ५. क.ग. मनिसन्धिश्च । ६. अ. कोलकान् । ७. अ.क.ग.ज. नवमेव । ८. अ.क.ग.ज. चुबुकात् । ९. अ. कूर्परान्ते च । क.ग. कूर्प्परान्ते च । १०. अ.क. अङ्गुष्टात् कपो° । ज. अङ्गुष्ठाग्रकपोलन्तु । This verse is missing in ग.

११. अ. स्वन्धमालकलम्बनम् । क. स्कन्धनालकाव° । १२. अ. अथोर्धबाहु° । क. ऊर्धबाहु° । ज. ऊर्ध्वे च बाहु° । १३. क. अधोक्षामतरम् । १४. क. मतम् । १५. अ. मणिसन्धी । क.ग. मनिसन्धे । ज. मणिसन्धिं । १६. अ. °कर्ण्णतालम्ब । १७. क. कपोलग्रञ्च लम्ब° । ग. कपोलग्रीवलम्बनम् । १८. अ. वक्त्रधारमुत्तु° । क. बक्त्राधारमुत्तु° । ग. वत्काधारामुत्तु° । १९. अ. सम्पूर्ण्णवदनञ्चापि । ज. सम्पूण्णमिव । २०. क.ग. श्यात् । २१. अ.क.ग. °सोभनम् । २२. अ. स्थितं निसन्न शयनं । क. निसिन्नो सय° । ग. निसन्नो सय° । २३. अ. त्रिबिम्बं । २४. अ. जिनक्षनम् । क. जिणुस्थादिलक्षणम् । Com. तादिसं जिनम् लक्षणम् । ग. जनस्थादिलक्षणं । Com. तादिकसं लक्षणम् । The forms तादिसं and तादिकसं betray influence of Pāli.

२५. अ. °दीर्गन्तु । क. पूर्ववत्तार° । २६. अ. तथाकुर्य्याच्च तादृशं । क. कुर्य्यात् तथेव पूर्ववत् । ग. कुर्यात् तथैव पूर्ववत् । ज. कुर्य्यात् तत्रैव ।

124. The distance from the armpit to the end of the elbow [shall be] eleven *kalās* (i.e., twenty-two *aṅgulas*), and that from the elbow to the wrist nine *kolakas*.

125. [The distance] from the nipple of the breast to the end of the elbow is declared to be six *kolakas*. One shall lay the eye-line from the end of the palm of the lower hand.

126. From the thumb [of the bent hand] hang the cheek, the neck and the lobe of the ear . The root of the upper arm [shall be] in line with (lit., equal to) the lower armpit (*kakṣāntara*).

127. The elevation of the root of the arm in relation to the wrist [shall be] two *aṅgulas*. The lobe of the upper ear hangs from the cheek up to the neck.

128. The height of the pillow [shall be] equivalent to the height of the face. The perfectly round face should look beautiful with all the [salutary] features.

129. The wise one shall accordingly determine as already stated the length and breadth of [all] images of such description in the three positions of standing, sedent and reclining.

सर्वलक्षणसम्पूर्णम्[१] पुण्यवृद्धिकरं शुभम्[२] ।
यदि हीनातिरिक्तञ्च सर्वभोगायुर्[३] नश्यति[४] ।।१३०।।

असुरराहुविधिं[५] कुर्यात् पादद्वारस्थितं वरम् ।
सर्वाभरणभूषितं[६] पुष्पमालाधरौ[७] करौ ।।१३१।।
त्रिवंकस्थायिकं[८] कुर्यात्[९] सर्वावयवशोभनम्[१०] ।।१३१½।।

इति गौतमीये[११] शारिपुत्रश्रुते[१२] बिम्बमानं[१३] समाप्तम् ।

---

१. क. °सम्पूर्ण्ण । ग. सर्वलक्षणसम्पन्न । २. अ. पुण्यबुद्धिसुभम्करम् । क. पुन्य° । ग. °करम् (भवेत्) सुभम् । ३. अ.क.ग.ज. °भोगायु । ४. अ.क. नष्टते । ग. णष्टते । क has colophon here. It is identical with that of ग.

५. अ. असुराराहुविधं । क.ग. °विधं । But both have विधिं in Com. ६. अ. °भूसित्वा । क.ग.ज. °भूषित्वा । ७. अ. पुष्फमाला° । ग omits करौ । ८. ग. त्रिवंकस्थिधिकं । ज. त्रिवंकस्थानकं । ९. अ. कुर्य्या । ग. कुय्या । १०. ग. °सोभणम् । ११. क.ग. गोतमीये । १२. ग. शारिपुत्त्रश्श्रुते । १३. ग. बिम्बमाण ।

130. [The image] endowed with all [beautiful] features [shall lead to] the accumulation of merits and bring welfare. If [its measurements are] shorter or longer than prescribed, all crops will perish and the life span [of the builder] will be shortened.

131. One shall make the noble figure of the Asura Rāhu standing at the doorstep adorned with all ornaments, endowed with two hands holding garlands, the body bent at knee joints, and beautiful with all [good] features.

Here end the *Bimbamāna* of the *Gautamīya* [-*śāstra*] as heard by Śāriputra.

Index